# DAILY AIR FRYER COOKBOOK

## 100 DELICIOUS EVERYDAY RECIPES FROM DINNER TO DESSERT FOR WHOLE FAMILY

## Martina Baker

# Table of Content

**Introduction** ............................................. 7

**Breakfast Recipes** ...................................... 10

1. Breakfast Granola
2. Pepper Stuffed Spinach
3. Parmesan Baked Eggs
4. Pepper Stuffed Spinach and Feta Eggs
5. Egg Stuffed Peppers and Cheese
6. Bacon and Egg Stuffed Peppers
7. Peppers and Eggs
8. Stuffed Spinach Parmesan
9. Brussels Hash
10. Vegetable Hash
11. Ham, Cheese and Mushroom Melt
12. Ham and Pepper Melt
13. Veggie Melt
14. Mozzarella Avocado Mix
15. Salsa Omelet
16. Salmon and Zucchini Salad
17. Parsley Avocado Salad
18. Bacon Omelet
19. Spinach and Asparagus Frittata
20. Asparagus Muffins
21. Coconut Eggs Mix
22. Eggplant and Avocado Salad
23. Peppers, Coconut and Eggs Mix
24. Yogurt Avocado Mix
25. Asparagus, Shrimp and Avocado Salad

26. Nutty Granola
27. Fruit and Nut Keto Granola
28. Strawberry and Nut Cereal

## Mains, Sides Recipes.............................50

1.  Sweet & Sour Chicken Skewer
2.  Green Stuffed Pepper
3.  Chipotle Green Beans
4.  Tomato and Cranberry Beans Pasta
5.  Mexican Casserole
6.  Scallions and Endives with Rice
7.  Cabbage and Tomatoes
8.  Lemony Endive Mix
9.  Eggplant and Tomato Sauce
10. Lentils and Spinach Casserole 64
11. Red Potatoes with Green Beans and Chutney
12.  Simple Italian Veggie Salad
13. Roasted Cauliflower with Nuts & Raisins
15. Spicy Herb Chicken Wings
16. Lamb Meatballs

## Seafood Recipes ...................................68

1.  Jalapeno Tuna Melt Cups
2.  Herbed Tuna Melt Cups
3.  Cajun Tuna Melt Cups
4.  Cheddar Tuna Melt Cups
5.  Fast Seared Scallops
6.  Spicy Cod Fish Sticks
7.  Italian Fish Sticks
8.  Lemon Pepper Fish Sticks

9. Salmon Fish Sticks
10.       Cajun Salmon Fish Sticks
11. Garlic Shrimp Bacon Bake
12. Gruyere Shrimp Bacon Bake
13. Garlic Shrimp Prosciutto Bake
14. Garlic Shrimp Tuna Bake

## Poultry and Meat Recipes ......................91

1. Cumin Chicken
2. Ground Chicken and Chilies
3. Chopped Chicken Olive Tomato Sauce
4. Chicken Thighs in Coconut Sauce, Nuts
5. Forest Guinea Hen
6. Chicken and Coriander Sauce
7. Turkey Chili
8. Chicken and Chickpeas
9. Turkey and Lentils
10.       Ground Turkey
Mix 12. Chicken and Bacon
Mix 13. Turkey and Mango
Mix 14. Herbed Turkey
15. Chicken Wings and Sprouts
16. Thyme Turkey

## Vegetables ...............................114

1.       Creamy Green Beans and Walnuts
2.       Garlic Corn
3.       Green Beans Salad
4.       Red Cabbage and Tomatoes
5.       Savoy Cabbage Sauté
6.       Turmeric Kale
7.       Lemon Fennel

8. Balsamic Kale
9. Coriander Endives
10. Cheesy Beets
11. Frying Potatoes
12. Lemon Tomatoes
13. Tomato and Green Beans
14. Tomato and Onions Mix
15. Kale Salad
16. Garlic Carrots

## Dessert and snacks .................................... 135

1. Sweet Zucchini Chips
2. Cucumber Chips
3. Dill and Onion Cucumber Chips
4. Smokey Cucumber Chips
5. Garlic Parmesan Cucumber Chips
6. Sea Salt and Black Pepper Cucumber Chips
7. Taco Cucumber Chips
8. Cayenne Zucchini Chips
9. Salt and Vinegar Zucchini Chips
10. Smoked Zucchini Chips
11. Yellow Zucchini Chips
12. Soft Pretzels
13. Soft Garlic Parmesan Pretzels
14. Soft Cinnamon Pretzels
15. Soft Pecan Pretzels
16. Soft Cheesy Pretzels

17.  Bread Pudding
18.  Coconut Cream and Cinnamon Pudding
19.  Plum Jam

# Introduction

There are many kinds of foods that you can cook using an air fryer, but there are also certain types that are not suited for it. Avoid cooking ingredients, which can be steamed, like beans and carrots. You also cannot fry foods covered in heavy batter in this appliance.

Aside from the above mentioned, you can cook most kinds of ingredients using an air fryer. You can use it to cook foods covered in light flour or breadcrumbs. You can cook a variety of vegetables in the appliance, such as cauliflower, asparagus, zucchini, kale, peppers, and corn on the cob. You can also use it to cook frozen foods and home prepared meals by following a different set of instructions for these purposes.

An air fryer also comes with another useful feature - the separator. It allows you to cook multiple dishes at a time. Use the separator to divide ingredients in the pan or basket. You have to make sure that all ingredients have the same temperature setting so that everything will cook evenly at the same time.

# The Benefits of Air fryer

It is important to note that air fried foods are still fried. Unless you've decided to eliminate the use of oils in cooking, you must still be cautious about the food you eat. Despite that, it clearly presents a better and healthier option than deep-frying. It helps you avoid unnecessary fats and oils, which makes it an ideal companion when you intend to lose weight. It offers a lot more benefits, which include the following:

- It is convenient and easy to use, plus, it's easy to clean.

- It doesn't give off unwanted smells when cooking.

- You can use it to prepare a variety of meals.

- It can withstand heavy cooking.

•　　　It is durable and made of metal and high-grade plastic.

•　　　Cooking using this appliance is not as messy as frying in a traditional way. You don't have to worry

about greasy spills and stains in the kitchen.

# Breakfast

Breakfast Granola

Preparation time: 10 minutes Cooking time: 18 minutes Servings: 12

INGREDIENTS

- 1 cup almonds, chopped finely
- ½ cup walnuts, chopped finely
- ½ cup hazelnuts, peeled, chopped finely
- 1 cup pecans, chopped finely
- 1/3 cup pumpkin seeds
- 1/3 cup hemp seeds
- 1/3 cup chia seeds
- ½ cup ground flaxseeds
- 1 tsp vanilla
- 1 egg white, whisked
- ¼ cup butter, melted

DIRECTIONS:

1. Preheat your air fryer to 325 degrees F.
2. Line your air fryer basket with parchment.

3.     Place the chopped nuts in a large bowl and then add the pumpkin seeds, hemp seeds, chia seeds and flaxseed. Toss well.

4.     Add the remaining ingredients and toss well.

5.     Pour the nut mix into the air fryer basket and bake for 18 minutes, tossing halfway through to bake evenly.

6.     Empty the granola onto a try and let cool completely. Enjoy with milk or own its own.

NUTRITION: Calories 342, Total Fat 32, Saturated Fat 22g, Total Carbs 7g, Net Carbs 2g, Protein 9g, Sugar 1G, Fiber 5g, Sodium 187mg, Potassium 54g

# Pepper Stuffed Spinach Parmesan Baked Eggs

Preparation time: 5 minutes

Cooking time: 14 minutes Servings: 2

## INGREDIENTS

- 4 eggs

- 2 Tbsp heavy cream
- 2 Tbsp frozen, chopped spinach, thawed
- 2 Tbsp grated parmesan cheese
- ½ tsp salt
- 1/8 tsp ground black pepper
- 1 large red pepper, cut in half vertically, seeds removed

## DIRECTIONS:

1. Preheat your air fryer to 330 degrees F.
2. Place red pepper halves in the air fryer basket and cook for 5 minutes.
3. In a small bowl, whisk together all the ingredients
4. Pour the eggs into the partially cooked peppers and bake for 7 minutes.
5. Enjoy straight out of the baking cup!

NUTRITION: Calories 189, Total Fat 11g, Saturated Fat 4g, Total Carbs 5g, Net Carbs 3g, Protein 14g, Sugar 2g, Fiber 2g, Sodium 134mg, Potassium 148g

# Pepper Stuffed Spinach and Feta Eggs

Preparation time: 5 minutes Cooking time: 14 minutes Servings: 2

## INGREDIENTS

- 4 eggs
- 2 Tbsp heavy cream
- 2 Tbsp frozen, chopped spinach, thawed
- ¼ cup feta crumbles
- ½ tsp salt
- 1/8 tsp ground black pepper
- 1 large red pepper, cut in half vertically, seeds removed

## DIRECTIONS:

1. Preheat your air fryer to 330 degrees F.

2. Place red pepper halves in the air fryer basket and cook for 5 minutes.

3. In a small bowl, whisk together all the ingredients

4.    Pour the eggs into the partially cooked peppers and bake for 7 minutes.

5.    Enjoy straight out of the baking cup!


NUTRITION: Calories 192, Total Fat 11g, Saturated Fat 6g, Total Carbs 5g, Net Carbs 3g, Protein 14g, Sugar 2g, Fiber 2g, Sodium 156mg, Potassium 148g

# Egg Stuffed Peppers and Cheese

Preparation time: 5 minutes Cooking time: 14 minutes Servings: 2

## INGREDIENTS

- 4 eggs
- 2 Tbsp heavy cream
- 2 Tbsp grated cheddar cheese
- 2 Tbsp grated parmesan cheese
- ½ tsp salt
- 1/8 tsp ground black pepper
- 1 large red pepper, cut in half vertically, seeds removed

## DIRECTIONS:

1. Preheat your air fryer to 330 degrees F.

2. Place red pepper halves in the air fryer basket and cook for 5 minutes.

3. In a small bowl, whisk together all the ingredients

4. Pour the eggs into the partially cooked peppers and bake for 7 minutes.

5. Enjoy straight out of the baking cup!

NUTRITION: Calories 178, Total Fat 16g, Saturated Fat 8g, Total Carbs 5g, Net Carbs 3g, Protein 10g, Sugar 2g, Fiber 2g, Sodium 134mg, Potassium 148g

## 53.    Bacon and Egg Stuffed Peppers

Preparation time: 5 minutes Cooking time: 14 minutes Servings: 2

INGREDIENTS

- 4 eggs
- 2 Tbsp heavy cream
- 2 Tbsp chopped cooked bacon
- 2 Tbsp grated cheddar cheese
- ½ tsp salt
- 1/8 tsp ground black pepper
- 1 large red pepper, cut in half vertically, seeds removed

DIRECTIONS:

1.    Preheat your air fryer to 330 degrees F.

2.    Place red pepper halves in the air fryer basket and cook for 5 minutes.

3.    In a small bowl, whisk together all the ingredients

4.    Pour the eggs into the partially cooked peppers and bake for 7 minutes.

5.    Enjoy straight out of the baking cup!


NUTRITION: Calories 210, Total Fat 19g, Saturated Fat 9, Total Carbs 9g, Net Carbs 4g, Protein 14g, Sugar 2g, Fiber 5g, Sodium 198mg, Potassium 148g

Peppers and Eggs Preparation time: 5 minutes
Cooking time: 14 minutes Servings: 2

INGREDIENTS

- 4 eggs
- 2 Tbsp heavy cream
- 1 jalapeno, sliced
- 2 Tbsp grated cheddar cheese
- ½ tsp salt
- 1/8 tsp ground black pepper
- 1 large red pepper, cut in half vertically, seeds removed

DIRECTIONS:
1.    Preheat your air fryer to 330 degrees F.
2.    Place red pepper halves in the air fryer basket and cook for 5 minutes.
3.    In a small bowl, whisk together all the ingredients
4.    Pour the eggs into the partially cooked peppers and bake for 7 minutes.
5.    Enjoy straight out of the baking cup!

NUTRITION: Calories 154, Total Fat 11g, Saturated Fat 4g, Total Carbs 5g, Net Carbs 3g, Protein 9g, Sugar 2g, Fiber 2g, Sodium 126mg, Potassium 154g

# Pepper Stuffed Spinach Parmesan Baked Eggs

Preparation time: 5 minutes Cooking time: 14 minutes Servings: 2

## INGREDIENTS

- 4 eggs
- 2 Tbsp heavy cream
- ¼ zucchini, sliced and chopped thinly
- 2 Tbsp grated parmesan cheese
- ½ tsp salt
- 1/8 tsp ground black pepper
- 1 large red pepper, cut in half vertically, seeds removed

## DIRECTIONS:

1. Preheat your air fryer to 330 degrees F.

2. Place red pepper halves in the air fryer basket and cook for 5 minutes.

3. In a small bowl, whisk together all the ingredients

4. Pour the eggs into the partially cooked peppers and bake for 7 minutes.

5. Enjoy straight out of the baking cup!

Brussels Hash Preparation time: 10 minutes
Cooking time: 25 minutes Servings: 4

INGREDIENTS

- 6 slices bacon, chopped, cooked
- ½ cup chopped white onion
- 1 pound Brussel sprouts, sliced in quarters
- ½ tsp salt
- ½ tsp ground black pepper
- 2 cloves garlic, minced
- 4 eggs, whisked

DIRECTIONS:

1. Preheat your air fryer to 350 degrees F.

2. Toss the bacon, onion, Brussels, salt, pepper and garlic together in a large bowl.

3.     Pour the mix into a seven inch pan that will fit in your air fryer basket.

4.     Place in the air fryer and cook for 15 minutes.

5.     Pour the whisked eggs in the basket and return the pan to the air fryer to cook for 10 more minutes.

6.     Mix well to break up the hash and enjoy while hot.

NUTRITION: Calories 238, Total Fat 12g, Saturated Fat 7g, Total Carbs 6g, Net Carbs 3g, Protein 12g, Sugar 1G, Fiber 3g, Sodium 189mg, Potassium 217G

57.     Zucchini Hash Preparation time: 10 minutes Cooking time: 25 minutes Servings: 4

INGREDIENTS

•     6 slices bacon, chopped, cooked

•     ½ cup chopped white onion

•     1     pound     shredded zucchini, water squeezed out

•     ½ tsp salt

•     ½ tsp ground black pepper

•     2 cloves garlic, minced

- 4 eggs, whisked

DIRECTIONS:

1.     Preheat your air fryer to 350 degrees F.

2.     Toss the bacon, onion, zucchini, salt, pepper and garlic together in a large bowl.

3.     Pour the mix into a seven inch pan that will fit in your air fryer basket.

4.     Place in the air fryer and cook for 15 minutes.

5.     Pour the whisked eggs in the basket and return the pan to the air fryer to cook for 10 more minutes.

6.     Mix well to break up the hash and enjoy while hot.

NUTRITION: Calories 215, Total Fat 11g, Saturated Fat 7g, Total Carbs 8g, Net Carbs 5g, Protein 10g, Sugar 3g, Fiber 3g, Sodium 189mg, Potassium 211G

Vegetable Hash Preparation time: 10 minutes Cooking time: 25 minutes Servings: 4

INGREDIENTS

- 6 slices bacon, chopped, cooked
- ½ cup chopped white onion
- 2 cups Brussel sprouts, sliced in quarters
- 2 cups diced green bell peppers
- ½ tsp salt
- ½ tsp ground black pepper
- 2 cloves garlic, minced
- 4 eggs, whisked

DIRECTIONS:

1. Preheat your air fryer to 350 degrees F.

2. Toss the bacon, onion, Brussels, bell peppers, salt, pepper and garlic together in a large bowl.

3. Pour the mix into a seven inch pan that will fit in your air fryer basket.

4. Place in the air fryer and cook for 15 minutes.

5. Pour the whisked eggs in the basket and return the pan to the air fryer to cook for 10 more minutes.

6.    Mix well to break up the hash and enjoy while hot.


NUTRITION: Calories 238, Total Fat 12g, Saturated Fat 7g, Total Carbs 6g, Net Carbs 3g, Protein 12g, Sugar 1G, Fiber 3g, Sodium 189mg, Potassium 217G

# Ham, Cheese and Mushroom Melt

Preparation time: 12 minutes Cooking time: 18 minutes Servings: 4

INGREDIENTS

- 2 Tbsp butter
- ½ pound sliced mushrooms
- 1 clove garlic, minced
- ¼ cup white onion, diced
- 1-16 oz ham steak, cooked
- ¼ cup cooked, crumbled bacon
- 1 Tbsp fresh parsley, chopped
- 1 cup grated gruyere cheese

DIRECTIONS:

1.      Preheat your air fryer to 350 degrees F.

2.      In a pan that will fit inside your air fryer, combine the butter and diced onion. Place in the preheated air fryer and cook for 5 minutes.

3.      Remove the pan from the air fryer and stir in the garlic and mushrooms. Return to the air fryer for another 5 minutes.

4.      Remove the pan again and add the ham steak, pushing it toward the bottom of the pan. Top with the bacon and grated cheese and place in the air fryer for another 8 minutes.

5.      Move the ham steak and pan contents to a plate, garnish with the parsley and serve while hot.

NUTRITION: Calories 352, Total Fat 22g, Saturated Fat 11G, Total Carbs 5g, Net Carbs 4g, Protein 34g, Sugar 2g, Fiber 1G, Sodium 1576mg, Potassium 387g

60.     Ham and Pepper Melt Preparation time: 10 minutes Cooking time: 18 minutes Servings: 4

INGREDIENTS

•       2 Tbsp butter

•       1 cup diced red peppers

- 1 clove garlic, minced

- ¼ cup white onion, diced
- 1-16 oz ham steak, cooked
- ¼ cup cooked, crumbled bacon
- 1 Tbsp fresh parsley, chopped
- 1 cup blue cheese

DIRECTIONS:

1.      Preheat your air fryer to 350 degrees F.

2.      In a pan that will fit inside your air fryer, combine the butter, bell peppers and diced onion. Place in the preheated air fryer and cook for 5 minutes.

3.      Remove the pan from the air fryer and stir in the garlic and mushrooms. Return to the air fryer for another 5 minutes.

4.      Remove the pan again and add the ham steak, pushing it toward the bottom of the pan. Top with the bacon and blue cheese and place in the air fryer for another 8 minutes.

5.      Move the ham steak and pan contents to a plate, garnish with the parsley and serve while hot.

Veggie Melt Preparation time: 10 minutes
Cooking time: 14 minutes Servings: 4

INGREDIENTS

- 2 Tbsp butter
- ½ pound sliced mushrooms
- 1 clove garlic, minced
- ¼ cup white onion, diced
- 1 cup diced green bell peppers
- 1 cup diced zucchini
- 1 cup chopped baby spinach
- 1 Tbsp fresh parsley, chopped
- 1 cup grated gruyere cheese

DIRECTIONS:

1. Preheat your air fryer to 350 degrees F.

2. In a pan that will fit inside your air fryer, combine the butter, bell pepper and diced onion.

Place in the preheated air fryer and cook for 5 minutes.

3.     Remove the pan from the air fryer and stir in the garlic, zucchini and mushrooms. Return to the air fryer for another 5 minutes.

4.     Remove the pan again and add the baby spinach and grated cheese and place in the air fryer for another 4 minutes.

5.     Move the ham steak and pan contents to a plate, garnish with the parsley and serve while hot.


NUTRITION: Calories 268, Total Fat 11g, Saturated Fat 7g, Total Carbs 8g, Net Carbs 5g, Protein 34g, Sugar 2g, Fiber 3g, Sodium 452mg, Potassium 254g

# Blueberry Breakfast Cake Preparation time: 10 minutes Cooking time: 24 minutes

Servings: 12

## INGREDIENTS

- 1 cup almond flour
- 1 Tbsp powdered stevia
- ¼ cup whole milk
- 1 egg

- ¼ tsp salt

- ¼ tsp ground cinnamon

- 2 tsp baking powder

- ½ cup frozen or fresh blueberries


DIRECTIONS:


1.	Preheat your air fryer to 350 degrees F.


2.	Spray a cake pan lightly with cooking spray. A seven inch pan will fit in most air fryers.

3.	In a large bowl, stir together the almond flour, stevia, salt, cinnamon, and baking powder.

4.	Add the eggs and milk and stir well.

5.	Fold in the blueberries.

6.	Pour the batter into the prepared pan and place into the air fryer basket and cook for 24 minutes or until a toothpick comes out cleanly when inserted into the center.

7.	Remove from the air fryer and let cool.

8.	Serve and enjoy!

NUTRITION: Calories 42, Total Fat 3g, Saturated Fat 1G, Total Carbs 3g, Net Carbs 2g, Protein 2g, Sugar 0g, Fiber 1G, Sodium 36mg, Potassium 68g

minutes Cooking time: 10 minutes Servings: 4

## INGREDIENTS

- 2 tablespoons butter, melted
- 1 cup avocado, peeled, pitted and cubed
- 1 cup black olives, pitted and sliced
- 1 cup mozzarella cheese, grated
- 1 tablespoon basil, chopped
- ½ teaspoon chili powder
- A pinch of salt and black pepper

## DIRECTIONS

1. Preheat your Air Fryer at 360 degrees F, grease with the butter, add the avocado, olives and the other ingredients, toss, cook for 10 minutes, divide into bowls and serve for breakfast.

NUTRITION: Calories 207, Fat 14, Fiber 3, Carbs 4, Protein 8

Salsa Omelet Preparation time: 5 minutes
Cooking time: 20 minutes Servings: 4

INGREDIENTS

- 8 eggs, whisked
- 1 cup mild salsa
- 4 scallions, chopped
- 1 tablespoon parsley, chopped
- Cooking spray
- ¼ cup mozzarella, shredded
- Salt and black pepper to the taste

DIRECTIONS

1. Heat up the air fryer at 360 degrees F, grease it with the cooking spray, add the eggs mixed with the salsa and the other ingredients, spread, cook for 20 minutes, divide between plates and serve.

NUTRITION: Calories 230, Fat 14, Fiber 3, Carbs 5, Protein 11

Salmon and Zucchini Salad Preparation time: 5 minutes Cooking time: 15 minutes

Servings: 4

## INGREDIENTS

- 1 cup zucchinis, roughly cubed
- 1 pound salmon fillets, boneless and cubed
- 1 tablespoon olive oil
- 1 cup baby spinach
- 1 cup cherry tomatoes
- ½ teaspoon chili powder
- 1 tablespoon chives, chopped

- Salt and black pepper to the taste

## DIRECTIONS

1. Heat up the Air Fryer with the oil at 360 degrees F, add the salmon and chili powder and cook for 5 minutes.

2.     Add the rest of the ingredients, toss, and cook for 10 more minutes, divide into bowls and serve for breakfast.


NUTRITION: Calories 240, Fat 14, Fiber 2, Carbs 5, Protein 11

Parsley Avocado Salad Preparation time: 5 minute Cooking time: 8 minutes Servings: 4

INGREDIENTS

- 1 cup avocado, peeled, pitted and roughly cubed
- 1 tablespoon lime juice
- 1 cup baby spinach
- 1 cup cucumber, roughly cubed
- 1 cup cherry tomatoes, halved
- 1 tablespoon parsley, chopped
- Cooking spray

DIRECTIONS

1. Grease the Air Fryer with the cooking spray, add the avocado, spinach and the other ingredients inside, and cook at 330 degrees F for 8 minutes.

2.    Divide the salad into bowls and serve for breakfast.

NUTRITION: Calories 240, Fat 13, Fiber 4, Carbs 6, Protein 9


Bacon Omelet Preparation


time: 5 minutes

Cooking time: 20 minutes Servings: 4

INGREDIENTS


- 2 tablespoons butter, melted
- 1 cup bacon, chopped
- 1 yellow onion, chopped
- 8 eggs, whisked
- ½ teaspoon turmeric powder
- ½ teaspoon sweet paprika
- 1 tablespoon chives, chopped
- Salt and black pepper to the taste

## DIRECTIONS

1.      Heat up the air fryer with the butter at 370 degrees F, add the bacon and cook for 5 minutes.

2.      Add the eggs and the other ingredients, spread into the machine, toss, cook for 15 minutes more, divide the omelet between plates and serve.

NUTRITION: Calories 200, Fat 4, Fiber 2, Carbs 4, Protein 4

39.    Spinach and Asparagus Frittata

Preparation time: 5 minutes Cooking time: 20 minutes Servings: 4

INGREDIENTS

- 1 tablespoon olive oil
- 1 cup baby spinach
- 1 cup asparagus, trimmed and sliced
- 8 eggs, whisked
- ½ teaspoon sweet paprika
- ½ cup heavy cream
- Salt and black pepper to the taste

DIRECTIONS

1.    In a bowl, combine the eggs with the spinach and the other ingredients except the oil and whisk.

2.    Grease the air fryer's pan with the oil, pour the frittata mix, spread, put the pan in the machine, cook at 380 degrees F for

20 minutes, divide between plates and serve for Breakfast.

NUTRITION: Calories 240, Fat 8, Fiber 3, Carbs 6,

40.    Asparagus Muffins Preparation time: 5 minutes Cooking time: 15 minutes Servings: 4

INGREDIENTS

- 3 eggs, whisked
- 1 cup asparagus, chopped
- Cooking spray
- 2 cups almond milk
- 1 cup almond flour
- 1 teaspoon baking soda
- 1 teaspoon baking powder
- 1 tablespoon cheddar, grated

DIRECTIONS

1.    In a bowl, combine the asparagus with the eggs and the other ingredients except the cooking spray and whisk.

2.    Grease a muffin pan that fits your air fryer with the cooking spray, divide the asparagus mix inside, put the pan in the air fryer, cook at 380

degrees F for 15 minutes, divide the muffins between plates and serve.

NUTRITION: Calories 210, Fat 12, Fiber 3, Carbs 5, Protein 8

41.    Coconut Eggs Mix Preparation time: 5 minutes Cooking time: 20 minutes Servings: 4

INGREDIENTS

- 1 cup coconut cream
- 8 eggs, whisked
- ½ cup coconut flesh, shredded
- ½ teaspoon turmeric powder
- 2 tablespoons chives, chopped
- A pinch of salt and black pepper
- 1 tablespoon mozzarella, shredded

DIRECTIONS

1.    In a bowl, combine the eggs with the cream, coconut flesh and the other ingredients and whisk

2.     Heat up the air fryer at 360 degrees F, add the eggs mix, stir, cook for 20 minutes shaking the machine halfway, divide between plates and serve for breakfast.

NUTRITION: Calories 220, Fat 14, Fiber 2, Carbs 5, Protein 11

42.    Eggplant and Avocado Salad

Preparation time: 10 minutes Cooking time: 10 minutes Servings: 4

INGREDIENTS

- 1 pound eggplant, cubed
- 1 cup avocado, peeled, pitted and cubed
- 1 cup cherry tomatoes, halved
- 1 cup kalamata olives, pitted and cubed
- 4 eggs, whisked
- 1 tablespoon cilantro, chopped

- Salt and black pepper to the taste
- 1 tablespoon chives, chopped

## DIRECTIONS

1. Heat up the air fryer with the cooking spray at 350 degrees F, add the eggplant, avocado and the other ingredients and cook for 10 minutes.

2. Divide the mix into bowls and serve for breakfast.

NUTRITION: Calories 241, Fat 11, Fiber 4, Carbs 5, Protein 12

43. Peppers, Coconut and Eggs Mix

Preparation time: 5 minutes Cooking time: 20 minutes Servings: 4

INGREDIENTS

- Cooking spray
- 1 cup green bell peppers, cut into strips
- 1 cup coconut flesh, shredded
- 8 eggs, whisked
- 2 spring onions, chopped
- 1 teaspoon oregano, dried
- Salt and black pepper to the taste
- 1 cup coconut cream

## DIRECTIONS

1.    In a bowl, combine the peppers with the coconut, eggs and the other ingredients except the cooking spray and whisk well.

2.    Grease the air fryer's pan with the cooking spray, add the peppers mix, put the pan in the machine and cook at 350 degrees F for 20 minutes.

3.    Divide between plates and serve for breakfast.

NUTRITION: Calories 251, Fat 16, Fiber 3, Carbs 6, Protein 11

44.    Yogurt Avocado Mix Preparation time: 5 minutes Cooking time: 20 minutes Servings: 4

## INGREDIENTS

- Salt and black pepper to the taste
- 2 cups Greek yogurt
- 1 cup avocado, peeled, pitted and cubed
- 4 eggs, whisked
- 1 tablespoon chives, chopped
- ½ teaspoon chili powder

## DIRECTIONS

1.	In a bowl, mix all the ingredients except the cooking spray and whisk well.

2.	Grease the air fryer's pan with the cooking spray, pour the avocado and yogurt mix, toss, and cook at 360 degrees F for 20 minutes.

3.	Divide between plates and serve for breakfast.

NUTRITION: Calories 221, Fat 14, Fiber 4, Carbs 6, Protein 11


45.	Asparagus, Shrimp and Avocado Salad


Preparation time: 5 minutes Cooking time: 10 minutes Servings: 4

## INGREDIENTS

- 1 bunch asparagus, trimmed and halved
- ½ pound shrimp, peeled and deveined
- 1 cup avocado, peeled, pitted and cubed
- 1 tablespoon olive oil
- 1 tablespoon lime juice
- ½ cup mild salsa

- A pinch of salt and black pepper

DIRECTIONS

1. In the air fryer, combine the asparagus with the shrimp and the other ingredients, toss and cook at 360 degrees F for 10 minutes.

2. Divide into bowls and serve for breakfast.

NUTRITION: Calories 200, Fat 5, Fiber 1, Carbs 4, Protein 5

46. Nutty Granola Preparation time: 10 minutes Cooking time: 18 minutes Servings: 12

INGREDIENTS

- 1 cup almonds, chopped finely
- ½ cup walnuts, chopped finely
- ½ cup hazelnuts, peeled, chopped finely
- 1 cup pecans, chopped finely
- 1/3 cup pumpkin seeds
- 1/3 cup hemp seeds
- ½ cup ground flaxseeds

- 1 tsp vanilla
- 1 egg white, whisked
- ¼ cup butter, melted

## DIRECTIONS:

1. Preheat your air fryer to 325 degrees F.

2. Line your air fryer basket with parchment.

3. Place the chopped nuts in a large bowl and then add the pumpkin seeds, hemp seeds and flaxseed. Toss well.

4. Add the remaining ingredients and toss well.

5. Pour the nut mix into the air fryer basket and bake for 18 minutes, tossing halfway through to bake evenly.

6. Empty the granola onto a try and let cool completely. Enjoy with milk or own its own.

NUTRITION: Calories 278, Total Fat 26, Saturated Fat 18g, Total Carbs 7g, Net Carbs 2g, Protein 7g, Sugar 1G, Fiber 5g, Sodium 187mg, Potassium 54g

47. Fruit and Nut Keto Granola Preparation time: 10 minutes Cooking time: 18 minutes

Servings: 12

INGREDIENTS

- 1 cup almonds, chopped finely
- ½ cup walnuts, chopped finely
- ½ cup hazelnuts, peeled, chopped finely
- ½ cup dried blueberries
- 1/3 cup pumpkin seeds
- 1/3 cup hemp seeds
- ½ cup ground flaxseeds
- 1 tsp vanilla
- 1 egg white, whisked
- ¼ cup butter, melted

DIRECTIONS:

1. Preheat your air fryer to 325 degrees F.

2. Line your air fryer basket with parchment.

3. Place the chopped nuts in a large bowl and then add the pumpkin seeds, hemp seeds, dried blueberries and flaxseed. Toss well.

4. Add the remaining ingredients and toss well.

5.    Pour the nut mix into the air fryer basket and bake for 18 minutes, tossing halfway through to bake evenly.

6.    Empty the granola onto a try and let cool completely. Enjoy with milk or own its own.


NUTRITION: Calories 328, Total Fat 26, Saturated Fat 18g, Total Carbs 13G, Net Carbs 8g, Protein 7g, Sugar 3g, Fiber 5g, Sodium 187mg, Potassium 54g

## 48. Strawberry and Nut Cereal Preparation time: 10 minutes Cooking time: 12 minutes

Servings: 12

## INGREDIENTS

- 1 cup almonds, chopped finely
- ½ cup walnuts, chopped finely
- ½ cup dried strawberries
- 1 cup pecans, chopped finely
- 1/3 cup pumpkin seeds
- 1/3 cup hemp seeds
- ½ cup ground flaxseeds
- 1 tsp vanilla
- 1 egg white, whisked
- ¼ cup butter, melted

## DIRECTIONS:

1. Preheat your air fryer to 325 degrees F.
2. Line your air fryer basket with parchment.

3.     Place the chopped nuts in a large bowl and then add the pumpkin seeds, hemp seeds and flaxseed. Toss well.

4.     Add the remaining ingredients and toss well.

5.     Pour the nut mix into the air fryer basket and bake for 18 minutes, tossing halfway through to bake evenly.

6.     Empty the granola onto a try and let cool completely. Enjoy with milk or own its own.


NUTRITION: Calories 298, Total Fat 27, Saturated Fat 18g, Total Carbs 11G, Net Carbs 6g, Protein 7g, Sugar 3g, Fiber 5g, Sodium 187mg, Potassium 54g

# Mains, Sides Recipes

127. Sweet & Sour Chicken Skewer

Cooking Time: 18 minutes Servings: 4

INGREDIENTS

- 1Lb. of chicken tenders
- ¼ teaspoon of pepper
- 4garlic cloves, minced
- 1½ tablespoons soy sauce

- 2tablespoons pineapple juice
- 1TAblespoon sesame oil
- ½ teaspoon ginger, minced

DIRECTIONS

1.   Preheat your air fryer to 390°Fahrenheit. Combine ingredients in a bowl, except for the chicken.

2.   Skewer the chicken tenders then place in a bowl and marinate for 2-hours.

3.   Add tenders to the air fryer and cook for 18-minutes.

4.    Serve hot!

## 128. Green Stuffed Peppers Cooking Time: 25 minutes Servings: 3

INGREDIENTS

- 3green bell peppers, tops, and seeds removed
- 1MEDium-sized onion, diced
- 1carrot, thinly diced
- 1SMAll cauliflower, shredded
- 1TEAspoon garlic powder
- 1TEAspoon coriander
- 1Teaspoon mixed spices
- 1TEAspoon Chinese five spice
- 1TAblespoon olive oil
- 3tablespoons any soft cheese
- 1Zucchini, thinly diced
- ¼ yellow pepper, thinly diced

## DIRECTIONS

1.      With the olive oil, sauté the onion in a wok over medium heat.

2.      Add the cauliflower and seasonings. Cook for 5-minutes, stir to combine.

3.      Add the vegetables (carrot, zucchini, yellow pepperand cook for an additional 5-minutes more.

4.      Fill each of the green peppers with 1-tablespoon of soft cheese.

5.      Then stuff them with cauliflower mixture.

6.      Cap stuffed peppers with the tops and cook in air fryer for 15-minutes at 390°Fahrenheit.

NUTRITION: Calories:        272, Total Fat:   12.7g, Carbs: 26g, Protein: 17g

116.   Scallions and Endives with Rice

Preparation time: 10 minutes Cooking time: 20 minutes Servings: 4

## INGREDIENTS

• 1TAblespoon olive oil

- 2scallions, chopped

- 3garlic cloves chopped
- 1TAblespoon ginger, grated
- 1TEAspoon chili sauce
- A pinch of salt and black pepper
- ½ cup white rice
- 1Cup veggie stock
- 3endives, trimmed and chopped

## DIRECTIONS

1. Grease a pan that fits your air fryer with the oil, add scallions, garlic, ginger, chili sauce, salt, pepper, rice, stock and endives, place in your air fryer, cover and cook at 365 degrees F for 20 minutes.

2. Divide casserole between plates and serve.

3. Enjoy!

NUTRITION: Calories 220, Fat 5, Fiber 8, Carbs 12, Protein 6

117. Cabbage and Tomatoes Preparation time: 10 minutes Cooking time: 12 minutes Servings: 4

INGREDIENTS

- 1TAblespoon olive oil
- 1Green cabbage head, chopped
- Salt and black pepper to the taste
- 15ounces canned tomatoes, chopped
- ½ cup yellow onion, chopped
- 2teaspoons turmeric powder

DIRECTIONS

1. In a pan that fits your air fryer, combine oil with green cabbage, salt, pepper, tomatoes, onion and turmeric, place in your air fryer and cook at 365 degrees F for 12 minutes.

2. Divide between plates and serve.

3. Enjoy!

NUTRITION: Calories 202, Fat 5, Fiber 8, Carbs 9, Protein 10

## 118. Lemony Endive Mix Preparation time: 10 minutes Cooking time: 10 minutes Servings: 4

INGREDIENTS

- 8endives, trimmed
- Salt and black pepper to the taste
- 3tablespoons olive oil
- Juice of ½ lemon
- 1TAblespoon tomato paste
- 2tablespoons parsley, chopped
- 1TEAspoon stevia

DIRECTIONS

1. In a bowl, combine endives with salt, pepper, oil, lemon juice, tomato paste, parsley and stevia, toss, place endives in your air fryer's basket and cook at 365 degrees F for 10 minutes.

2. Divide between plates and serve.

3. Enjoy!

NUTRITION: Calories 160, Fat 4, Fiber 7, Carbs 9, Protein 4

## 119.   Eggplant and Tomato Sauce

Preparation time: 10 minutes Cooking time: 12 minutes Servings: 2

INGREDIENTS

- 4cups eggplant, cubed
- 1TAblespoon olive oil
- 1TAblespoon garlic powder
- A pinch of salt and black pepper

- 3garlic cloves, minced
- 1Cup tomato sauce

DIRECTIONS

1.   In a pan that fits your air fryer, combine eggplant cubes with oil, garlic, salt, pepper, garlic powder and tomato sauce, toss, place in your air fryer and cook at 370 degrees F for 12 minutes.

2.   Divide between plates and serve.

3.   Enjoy!

NUTRITION: Calories 250, Fat 7, Fiber 5, Carbs 10, Protein 4

120.  Spiced Brown Rice with Mung Beans

Preparation time: 10 minutes Cooking time: 16 minutes Servings: 2

INGREDIENTS

- ½ teaspoon olive oil
- ½ cup brown rice, cooked
- ½ cup mung beans
- ½ teaspoon cumin seeds
- ½ cup red onion, chopped
- 2tomatoes, chopped
- 1SMAll ginger piece, grated
- 4garlic cloves, minced
- 1TEAspoon coriander, ground
- ½ teaspoon turmeric powder
- A pinch of cayenne pepper
- ½ teaspoon garam masala
- 1Cup veggie stock

- Salt and black pepper to the taste

- 1TEAspoon lemon juice

## DIRECTIONS

1.    In your blender, mix tomato with garlic, onions, ginger, salt, pepper, garam

masala, cayenne, coriander and turmeric and pulse really well.

2.    In a pan that fits your air fryer, combine oil with blended tomato mix, mung beans, rice, stock, cumin and lemon juice, place in your air fryer and cook at 365 degrees F for 16 minutes.

3.    Divide everything between plates and serve.

4.    Enjoy!

NUTRITION: Calories 200, Fat 6, Fiber 7, Carbs 10, Protein 8

## 121. Lentils and Spinach Casserole

Preparation time: 10 minutes Cooking time: 16 minutes Servings: 3

### INGREDIENTS

- 1TEAspoon olive oil
- 1/3 cup canned brown lentils, drained
- 1SMAll ginger piece, grated
- 4garlic cloves, minced
- 1Green chili pepper, chopped
- 2tomatoes, chopped
- ½ teaspoon garam masala
- ½ teaspoon turmeric powder
- 2potatoes, cubed
- Salt and black pepper to the taste
- ¼ teaspoon cardamom, ground
- ¼ teaspoon cinnamon powder
- 6ounces spinach leaves

### DIRECTIONS

1.    In a pan that fits your air fryer combine oil with canned lentils, ginger, garlic, chili pepper, tomatoes, garam masala, turmeric, potatoes, salt, pepper, cardamom, cinnamon and spinach, toss, place in your air fryer and cook at 356 degrees F for 16 minutes.

2.    Divide casserole between plates and serve.

3.    Enjoy!

NUTRITION: Calories 250, Fat 3, Fiber 11, Carbs 16, Protein 10

122.   Red Potatoes with Green Beans and Chutney

Preparation time: 10 minutes Cooking time: 14 minutes Servings: 4

INGREDIENTS

- 2pounds red potatoes, cubed
- 1Cup green beans
- 1Cup carrots, shredded
- 16ounces canned chickpeas, drained
- 2tablespoons olive oil

- 1TEAspoon coriander seeds
- 1ANd ½ teaspoons cumin seeds
- 1ANd ½ teaspoons garam masala
- ½ teaspoon mustard seeds
- 1TEAspoon garlic, minced

For the chutney:

- ¼ cup water
- ½ cup mint
- ½ cup cilantro
- 1SMAll ginger piece, grated
- 2teaspoons lime juice
- A pinch of salt

## DIRECTIONS

1. In a baking dish that fits your air fryer, combine oil with potatoes, green beans, carrots, chickpeas, coriander, cumin, garam masala, mustard seeds and garlic, place in your air fryer and cook at 365 degrees F for 20 minutes.

2.    In your blender, mix water with mint, cilantro, ginger, lime juice and salt and pulse really well.

3.    Divide potato mix between plates, add mint chutney on top and serve.

4.    Enjoy!

NUTRITION: Calories 241, Fat 4, Fiber 7, Carbs

11, Protein 6

123.  Simple Italian Veggie Salad Preparation time: 10 minutes Cooking time: 10 minutes

Servings: 8

INGREDIENTS

- 1ANd ½ cups tomatoes, chopped
- 3cups eggplant, chopped
- 2teaspoons capers
- Cooking spray
- 3garlic cloves, minced
- 2teaspoons balsamic vinegar
- 1TAblespoon basil, chopped
- A pinch of salt and black pepper

## DIRECTIONS

1.    Grease a pan that fits your air fryer with cooking spray, add tomatoes, eggplant, capers, garlic, salt and pepper, place in your air fryer and cook at 365 degrees F for 10 minutes.

2.    Divide between plates, drizzle balsamic vinegar all over, sprinkle basil and serve cold.

3.    Enjoy!

NUTRITION: Calories 171, Fat 3, Fiber 1, Carbs 8, Protein 12

## 124.   Roasted Cauliflower with Nuts & Raisins

Servings: 4

## INGREDIENTS

• 1SMAll cauliflower head, cut into florets

• 2tablespoons pine nuts, toasted

- 2tablespoons raisins, soak in boiling water and drain
- 1TEAspoon curry powder
- ½ teaspoon sea salt
- 3tablespoons olive oil

## DIRECTIONS

1. Preheat your air fryer to 320°Fahrenheit for 2-minutes. Add ingredients into a bowl and toss to combine. Add the cauliflower mixture to air fryer basket and cook for 15-minutes.

NUTRITION: Calories: 264, Total Fat: 26g, Carbs: 8g, Protein: 2g

125. Spicy Herb Chicken Wings Cooking Time: 15 minutes Servings: 6

## INGREDIENTS

- 4lbs. chicken wings
- ½ tablespoon ginger
- 2tablespoons vinegar
- 1Fresh lime juice
- 1TAblespoon olive oil

- 2tablespoons soy sauce
- 6garlic cloves, minced
- 1Habanero, chopped
- ¼ teaspoon cinnamon
- ½ teaspoon sea salt

## DIRECTIONS

1. Preheat your air fryer to 390°Fahrenheit.
2. Add ingredients to a large bowl and combine well.

3. Place chicken wings into the marinade mix and store in the fridge for 2 hours.
4. Add chicken wings to the air fryer and cook for 15-minutes.
5. Serve hot!

NUTRITION: Calories: 673, Total Fat: 29g, Carbs: 9g, Protein: 39g

## 126. Lamb Meatballs Cooking Time: 15 minutes Servings: 4

INGREDIENTS

- 1Lb. ground lamb
- 1EGg white
- ½ teaspoon sea salt
- 2tablespoons parsley, fresh, chopped
- 1TAblespoon coriander, chopped
- 2garlic cloves, minced
- 1TAblespoon olive oil
- 1TAblespoon mint, chopped

DIRECTIONS

1.Preheat your air fryer to 320°Fahrenheit. 2.Add all the ingredients in a mixing bowl and combine well.

3. Shape small meatballs from the mixture and place them in air fryer basket and cook for 15-minutes.

4. Serve hot!

# SEAFOOD
# RECIPES

## 357. Jalapeno Tuna Melt Cups

Cooking time: 20 minutes Servings: 7

INGREDIENTS

- 5oz canned tuna, drained
- 2eggs
- ¼ cup sour cream
- ¼ cup mayonnaise
- ¾ cup shredded cheddar cheese
- ¾ cup pepper jack cheese
- ¼ tsp salt
- ¼ tsp ground black pepper
- 1Tbsp parsley, chopped
- ½ cup jalapeno slices

DIRECTIONS:

1.     Preheat your air fryer to 325 degrees F and grease a muffin tin or individual muffin cups-whichever option fits in your air fryer better.

2.     In a large bowl, combine the tuna, mayonnaise, sour cream, both kinds of grated cheese, parsley, jalapeno slices, salt, and pepper.

3.     Scoop the mix into the prepared muffin tin, filling each cup to the top.

4.     Bake in the air fryer for 20 minutes or until the tops are golden brown.

5.     Place on a slice of keto bread, serve with keto crackers or enjoy plain with a spoon!

NUTRITION: Calories 167, Total Fat 13g, Saturated Fat 3, Total Carbs 2g, Net Carbs 1G, Protein 9g, Sugar 2g, Fiber 0g, Sodium 321MG, Potassium 197g

358.   Herbed Tuna Melt Cups Preparation time: 10 minutes Cooking time: 20 minutes Servings: 7

Preparation time: 10 minutes

INGREDIENTS

- 5oz canned tuna, drained

- 2eggs

- ¼ cup sour cream

- ¼ cup mayonnaise

- ¾ cup shredded cheddar cheese

- ¾ cup pepper jack cheese

- ¼ tsp salt

- ¼ tsp ground black pepper

- 1TBsp parsley, chopped

- 1TSP fresh chopped rosemary

- 1TSP fresh chopped basil

DIRECTIONS:

1. Preheat your air fryer to 325 degrees F and grease a muffin tin or individual muffin cups-whichever option fits in your air fryer better.

2. In a large bowl, combine the tuna, mayonnaise, sour cream, both kinds of grated cheese, parsley, rosemary, basil, salt, and pepper.

3. Scoop the mix into the prepared muffin tin, filling each cup to the top.

4. Bake in the air fryer for 20 minutes or until the tops are golden brown.

5. Place on a slice of keto bread, serve with keto crackers or enjoy plain with a spoon!

NUTRITION: Calories 163, Total Fat 13g, Saturated Fat 3, Total Carbs 1G, Net Carbs 1G, Protein 9g, Sugar 1G, Fiber 0g, Sodium 325mg, Potassium 197g

359. Cajun Tuna Melt Cups Preparation time: 10 minutes Cooking time: 20 minutes Servings: 7

INGREDIENTS

- 5oz canned tuna, drained

- 2eggs
- ¼ cup sour cream
- ¼ cup mayonnaise
- ¾ cup shredded cheddar cheese
- ¾ cup pepper jack cheese
- ¼ tsp salt
- ½ tsp Cajun seasoning
- 1Tbsp parsley, chopped

DIRECTIONS:

1. Preheat your air fryer to 325 degrees F and grease a muffin tin or individual muffin cups- whichever option fits in your air fryer better.

2. In a large bowl, combine the tuna, mayonnaise, sour cream, both kinds of grated cheese, parsley, Cajun seasoning, salt, and pepper.

3. Scoop the mix into the prepared muffin tin, filling each cup to the top.

4. Bake in the air fryer for 20 minutes or until the tops are golden brown.

5. Place on a slice of keto bread, serve with keto crackers or enjoy plain with a spoon!


NUTRITION: Calories 161, Total Fat 13G, Saturated Fat 3, Total Carbs 1G, Net Carbs 1G, Protein 9g, Sugar 1G, Fiber 0g, Sodium 321mg, Potassium 197g


360. Cheddar Tuna Melt Cups Preparation time: 10 minutes Cooking time: 20 minutes Servings: 7

INGREDIENTS


• 5oz canned tuna, drained

• 2eggs

• ¼ cup sour cream

• ¼ cup mayonnaise

- 1½ cups shredded cheddar cheese
- ¼ tsp salt

- ¼ tsp ground black pepper
- 1Tbsp parsley, chopped

## DIRECTIONS

1.  Preheat your air fryer to 325 degrees F and grease a muffin tin or individual muffin cups-whichever option fits in your air fryer better.

2.  In a large bowl, combine the tuna, mayonnaise, sour cream, cheese, parsley, salt and pepper.

3.  Scoop the mix into the prepared muffin tin, filling each cup to the top.

4.  Bake in the air fryer for 20 minutes or until the tops are golden brown.

5.  Place on a slice of keto bread, serve with keto crackers or enjoy plain with a spoon!

NUTRITION: Calories 160, Total Fat 13g, Saturated Fat 3, Total Carbs 1G, Net Carbs 1G, Protein 9g, Sugar 1G, Fiber 0g, Sodium 321mg, Potassium 197g

345. Spicy Cod Fish Sticks Preparation time: 10 minutes Cooking time: 10 minutes Servings: 4

## INGREDIENTS

- 1POund cod
- ¼ cup mayonnaise
- 2bsp mustard
- ½ tsp salt
- ½ tsp ground cayenne pepper
- 1½ cups ground pork rinds
- 2Tbsp whole milk

## DIRECTIONS:

1.      Preheat your air fryer to 400 degrees F and line your air fryer tray with foil and spray with cooking grease.

2.      Dry the cod filets by patting with a paper towel. Cut the fish into strips about 1 inch wide and two inches long.

3.      In a small bowl, combine the mustard, mayo and milk and stir together well.

4.      In a separate bowl, combine the ground pork rinds, salt and cayenne pepper.

5.　　Dip the fish strips into the mayonnaise mix and then into the pork rind mix, coating the fish completely. Place it on the prepared tray when done and repeat with the remaining fish sticks.

6.　　Place the tray in the air fryer and bake the fish for 5 minutes, flip and bake for another 5 minutes Servings while hot!

NUTRITION: Calories 264, Total Fat 16g, Saturated Fat 5g, Total Carbs 1G, Net Carbs 0g, Protein 26g, Sugar 0g, Fiber 1G, Sodium 679mg, Potassium 68g

346. Italian Fish Sticks Preparation time: 10 minutes Cooking time: 10 minutes Servings: 4

INGREDIENTS

- 1POund cod
- ¼ cup mayonnaise
- 2Tbsp mustard
- ½ tsp salt
- 1TSP Italian seasoning
- ½ tsp ground black pepper
- 1½ cups ground pork rinds
- 2Tbsp whole milk

DIRECTIONS:

1.      Preheat your air fryer to 400 degrees F and line your air fryer tray with foil and spray with cooking grease.

2.      Dry the cod filets by patting with a paper towel. Cut the fish into strips about 1 inch wide and two inches long.

3.      In a small bowl, combine the mustard, mayo and milk and stir together well.

4.      In a separate bowl, combine the ground pork rinds, salt, Italian seasoning and pepper.

5.      Dip the fish strips into the mayonnaise mix and then into the pork rind mix, coating the fish completely. Place it on the prepared tray when done and repeat with the remaining fish sticks.

6.      Place the tray in the air fryer and bake the fish for 5 minutes, flip and bake for another  5
        minutes Servings while hot!

NUTRITION: Calories 283, Total Fat 16g, Saturated Fat 5g, Total Carbs 1G, Net Carbs 0g, Protein 26g, Sugar 0g, Fiber 1G, Sodium 683mg, Potassium 68g

347. Lemon Pepper Fish Sticks Preparation time: 10 minutes Cooking time: 10 minutes

Servings: 4

## INGREDIENTS

- 1POund cod
- ¼ cup mayonnaise
- 2Tbsp mustard
- ½ tsp salt
- 1TSP lemon pepper seasoning
- 1½ cups ground pork rinds
- 2Tbsp whole milk

## DIRECTIONS:

1.    Preheat your air fryer to 400 degrees F and line your air fryer tray with foil and spray with cooking grease.

2.    Dry the cod filets by patting with a paper towel. Cut the fish into strips about 1 inch wide and two inches long.

3.    In a small bowl, combine the mustard, mayo and milk and stir together well.

4.    In a separate bowl, combine the ground pork rinds, lemon pepper and salt.

5.    Dip the fish strips into the mayonnaise mix and then into the pork rind mix, coating the fish completely. Place it on

the prepared tray when done and repeat with the remaining fish sticks.

6.    Place the tray in the air fryer and bake the fish for 5 minutes, flip and bake for another   5
       minutes Servings while hot!

NUTRITION: Calories 265, Total Fat 16g, Saturated Fat 5g, Total Carbs 1G, Net Carbs 0g, Protein 26g, Sugar 0g, Fiber 1G, Sodium 682mg, Potassium 69g

348. Salmon Fish Sticks Preparation time: 10 minutes Cooking time: 10 minutes Servings: 4

INGREDIENTS

- 1POund salmon filets
- ¼ cup mayonnaise
- 2Tbsp mustard
- ½ tsp salt
- ½ tsp ground black pepper
- 1½ cups ground pork rinds
- 2Tbsp whole milk

DIRECTIONS:

1.     Preheat your air fryer to 400 degrees F and line your air fryer tray with foil and spray with cooking grease.

2.     Dry the salmon filets by patting with a paper towel. Cut the fish into strips about 1 inch wide and two inches long.

3.     In a small bowl, combine the mustard, mayo and milk and stir together well.

4.     In a separate bowl, combine the ground pork rinds, salt and pepper.

5.     Dip the fish strips into the mayonnaise mix and then into the pork rind mix, coating the fish completely. Place it on the prepared tray when done and repeat with the remaining fish sticks.

6.     Place the tray in the air fryer and bake the fish for 5 minutes, flip and bake for another  5
        minutes Servings while hot!

NUTRITION: Calories 282, Total Fat 18g, Saturated Fat 5g, Total Carbs 1G, Net Carbs 0g, Protein 27g, Sugar 0g, Fiber 1G, Sodium 664mg, Potassium 68g

349.  Cajun Salmon Fish Sticks Preparation time: 10 minutes Cooking time: 10 minutes Servings: 4

# INGREDIENTS

- 1POund salmon
- ¼ cup mayonnaise
- 2Tbsp mustard
- ½ tsp salt
- 1TSP Cajun seasoning
- 1½ cups ground pork rinds
- 2Tbsp whole milk

# DIRECTIONS:

1. Preheat your air fryer to 400 degrees F and line your air fryer tray with foil and spray with cooking grease.

2. Dry the salmon filets by patting with a paper towel. Cut the fish into strips about 1 inch wide and two inches long.

3. In a small bowl, combine the mustard, mayo and milk and stir together well.

4. In a separate bowl, combine the ground pork rinds, Cajun seasoning, and salt.

5. Dip the fish strips into the mayonnaise mix and then into the pork rind mix, coating the fish

completely. Place it on the prepared tray when done and repeat with the remaining fish sticks.

6.     Place the tray in the air fryer and bake the fish for 5 minutes, flip and bake for

another 5 minutes Servings while hot!

NUTRITION: Calories 288, Total Fat 18g, Saturated Fat 5g, Total Carbs 1G, Net Carbs 0g, Protein 27g, Sugar 0g, Fiber 1G, Sodium 676mg, Potassium 68g

352. Garlic Shrimp Bacon Bake Preparation time: 10 minutes Cooking time: 8 minutes

Servings: 4

## INGREDIENTS

- ¼ cup butter
- 2Tbsp minced garlic
- 1POund shrimp, peeled and cleaned
- ¼ tsp ground black pepper
- ½ cup cooked, chopped bacon
- 1/3 cup heavy cream
- ¼ cup parmesan cheese

## DIRECTIONS:

1.     Preheat your air fryer to 400 degrees F and grease an 8x8 inch baking pan.

2.     Add the butter and shrimp to the pan and place in the air fryer for 3 minutes. Remove the pan from the air fryer.

3.     Add the remaining ingredients to the pan and return to the air fryer to cook for another 5 minutes. The mix should be bubbling and the shrimp should be pink.

4.     Serve with zucchini noodles or enjoy plain.

NUTRITION: Calories 350, Total Fat 27g, Saturated Fat 15g, Total Carbs 3g, Net Carbs 3g, Protein 36g, Sugar 0g, Fiber 0g, Sodium 924mg, Potassium 16G

353. Gruyere Shrimp Bacon Bake

Preparation time: 10 minutes Cooking time: 10 minutes Servings: 4

INGREDIENTS

•     ¼ cup butter

- 2Tbsp minced garlic
- 1POund shrimp, peeled and cleaned
- ¼ tsp ground black pepper
- ½ cup cooked, chopped bacon
- 1/3 cup heavy cream
- ¼ cup parmesan cheese
- ½ cup gruyere cheese, grated

## DIRECTIONS:

1. Preheat your air fryer to 400 degrees F and grease an 8x8 inch baking pan.

2. Add the butter and shrimp to the pan and place in the air fryer for 3 minutes. Remove the pan from the air fryer.

3. Add the remaining ingredients to the pan and return to the air fryer to cook for another 5 minutes. The mix should be bubbling and the shrimp should be pink.

4. Sprinkle the gruyere over the shrimp and return to the air fryer for another 2 minutes to brown the top of the cheese.

5. Serve with zucchini noodles or enjoy plain.

NUTRITION: Calories 410, Total Fat 32g, Saturated Fat 18g, Total Carbs 4g, Net Carbs 3g, Protein 38g, Sugar 0g, Fiber 0g, Sodium 988mg, Potassium 24g

354. Cajun Shrimp Bacon Bake Preparation time: 10 minutes Cooking time: 10 minutes

Servings: 4

## INGREDIENTS

- ¼ cup butter
- 2Tbsp minced garlic
- 1POund shrimp, peeled and cleaned
- ½ tsp Cajun seasoning
- ½ cup cooked, chopped bacon
- 1/3 cup heavy cream
- ¼ cup parmesan cheese

## DIRECTIONS:

1. Preheat your air fryer to 400 degrees F and grease an 8x8 inch baking pan.

2. Add the butter and shrimp to the pan and place in the air fryer for 3 minutes. Remove the pan from the air fryer.

3. Add the remaining ingredients to the pan and return to the air fryer to cook for another 5 minutes. The mix should be bubbling and the shrimp should be pink.

4. Serve with zucchini noodles or enjoy plain.

NUTRITION: Calories 352, Total Fat 27g, Saturated Fat 15g, Total Carbs 3g, Net Carbs 3g, Protein 36g, Sugar 0g, Fiber 0g, Sodium 930mg, Potassium 18g

355. Garlic Shrimp Prosciutto Bake


Preparation time: 10 minutes Cooking time: 10 minutes Servings: 4

INGREDIENTS


- ¼ cup butter

- 2Tbsp minced garlic

- 1POund shrimp, peeled and cleaned

- ¼ tsp ground black pepper

- 2oz thinly sliced, shredded prosciutto

- 1/3 cup heavy cream

- ¼ cup parmesan cheese

## DIRECTIONS:

1.    Preheat your air fryer to 400 degrees F and grease an 8x8 inch baking pan.

2.    Add the butter and shrimp to the pan and place in the air fryer for 3 minutes. Remove the pan from the air fryer.

3.    Add the remaining ingredients to the pan and return to the air fryer to cook for another 5 minutes. The mix should be bubbling and the shrimp should be pink.


4.    Serve with zucchini noodles or enjoy plain.

NUTRITION: Calories 358, Total Fat 27g, Saturated Fat 15g, Total Carbs 3g, Net Carbs 3g, Protein 36g, Sugar 0g, Fiber 0g, Sodium 1026mg, Potassium 16G

356. Garlic Shrimp Tuna Bake Preparation time: 10 minutes Cooking time: 10 minutes Servings: 4

INGREDIENTS

- ¼ cup butter
- 2Tbsp minced garlic
- 1POund shrimp, peeled and cleaned
- ¼ tsp ground black pepper
- 1TIN canned tuna, drained well
- 1/3 cup heavy cream
- ¼ cup parmesan cheese

DIRECTIONS:

1. Preheat your air fryer to 400 degrees F and grease an 8x8 inch baking pan.

2. Add the butter and shrimp to the pan and place in the air fryer for 3 minutes. Remove the pan from the air fryer.

3. Add the remaining ingredients to the pan and return to the air fryer to cook for another 5 minutes. The mix should be bubbling and the shrimp should be pink.

4. Serve with zucchini noodles or enjoy plain.

NUTRITION: Calories 376, Total Fat 30g, Saturated Fat 15g, Total Carbs 3g, Net Carbs 3g, Protein 43g, Sugar 0g, Fiber 0g, Sodium 924mg, Potassium 16G

# Poultry Recipes

426. Cumin Chicken Preparation time: 10 minutes Cooking time: 30 minutes Servings: 4

INGREDIENTS

- 1TAblespoon olive oil

- 1POund chicken breast, skinless, boneless and cubed
- Salt and black pepper to the taste
- 1TEAspoon cumin, ground
- 3spring onions, chopped
- ½ cup tomato sauce
- 1Cup chicken stock
- ½ tablespoon chives, chopped

DIRECTIONS:

1.     In the air fryer's pan, mix the chicken with the oil and the other ingredients and toss.

2.     Introduce the pan in the air fryer and cook at 380 degrees F for 30 minutes.

3.     Divide everything between plates and serve.

NUTRITION: Calories 261, Fat 11, Fiber 6, Carbs 19, Protein 17

427. Ground Chicken and Chilies Preparation time: 10 minutes Cooking time: 30 minutes

Servings: 4

INGREDIENTS

- 2pounds chicken breast, skinless, boneless and ground
- 1Yellow onion, minced
- 1TEAspoon chili powder
- 1TEAspoon sweet paprika
- Salt and black pepper to the taste
- 1TAblespoon olive oil
- 4ounces canned green chilies, chopped
- A handful parsley, chopped

## DIRECTIONS

1.    In the air fryer's pan, mix the chicken with the onion, chili powder and the other ingredients, introduce the pan in the air

fryer and cook at 370 degrees F for 30 minutes.

2.    Divide into bowls and serve.

## 428.  Chopped Chicken Olive Tomato Sauce

Preparation time: 10 minutes Cooking time: 30 minutes Servings: 4

## INGREDIENTS

- 500 g chicken cutlet
- 2minced shallots+1 degermed garlic clove
- 75 g of tomato sauce + 15 g of 30% liquid cream
- 1Bay leaf+salt+pepper+1 tsp Provence herbs
- 20pitted green and black olives

DIRECTION:

1.      Cut the chicken cutlets into strips and put them in the fryer basket with the garlic and the shallots. Do not put oil. Salt/pepper.

2.      Set the timer and the temperature to 10- 12 minutes at 200°C

3.      Add the tomato sauce, the cream, the olives, the bay leaf, and the Provence herbs. Salt if necessary. Mix with a wooden spoon.

4.      Close the air fryer and program 20 minutes at 180°C.

5.      Eat hot with rice or pasta.

NUTRITION: Calories 220.2 Fat 7.0 g Carbohydrate 8.5 g Sugars 4.5 g Protein28.9 g Cholesterol 114.8 mg

### 429. Chicken Thighs in Coconut Sauce, Nuts

Preparation time: 10 minutes Cooking time: 30 minutes

Servings: 4

INGREDIENTS

- 8skinless chicken thighs

- 2chopped onions

- 25ml of coconut cream + 100 ml of coconut milk

- 4tbsp coconut powder + 1 handful of dried fruit mix+ 5 dried apricots, diced + a few cashew nuts and almonds

- Fine salt + pepper

DIRECTION:

1. Put the onions, chopped with the chicken thighs, in the air fryer (without oil). Add salt and pepper. Program 10 minutes at 200°C.

2. Stir alone with a wooden spoon.

3. Add coconut cream and milk, coconut powder, dried fruits, and apricots. Get out if necessary. Continue cooking by programming 20 minutes at 200°C. You don't have anything to do; it cooks alone, without any problem.

4. With the tongs, remove the bowl and serve hot with rice, vegetables, Chinese noodles............... A delight. Perfect kitchen

NUTRITION: Calories 320.4 Fat 11.6 g Carbohydrate 9.0 g Sugars 2.1 g Protein44.0 g Cholesterol 102.7 mg

430. Forest Guinea Hen Preparation time: about 15 minutes Cooking time: 1 h 15 - 1 h 30 Servings: 4

INGREDIENTS

• A beautiful guinea fowl farm weighing 1 to 1.5 kilos

• 100g of dried or fresh porcini mushrooms according to the season

• 8large potatoes Béa

• 1PLate

• 2cloves of garlic

• 1SHallot

- Chopped parsley

- A pinch of butter

- Vegetable oil

- Salt and pepper

DIRECTION:

1. Put the dried mushrooms in water to rehydrate them or simply clean them if they are fresh porcini mushrooms. Peel the potatoes and cut them finely. Chop the garlic and parsley and set aside.

2. Prepare the guinea fowl by cutting the neck and removing all the giblets inside. Garnish with stuffed dough, garlic cloves and parsley.

3. Place guinea fowls in the air fryer at 2000C without oil of sufficient capacity. Simply add the butter knob and a tablespoon of cooking oil. Allow approximately one hour of cooking per kilo, so you will have to check after a certain period.

4. When the guinea fowl is ready, prepare the porcini mushrooms in the oil-free fryer by adding the shallot. This preparation is very fast, and you should not forget salt and pepper.

5. When everything is ready, place each of the preparations in the air fryer, sprinkle with the cooking juices and cook for another 15 minutes.

6. Serve hot to enjoy all the flavors of the dish.

NUTRITION: Calories 110 Fat 2.5g Carbohydrate 0g Sugars 0g Protein 21G Cholesterol 63mg

## 415. Chicken and Coriander Sauce

Preparation time: 10 minutes Cooking time: 25 minutes Servings: 4

INGREDIENTS

- 2pounds chicken breast, skinless, boneless and sliced
- 1Cup cilantro, chopped
- Juice of 1 lime
- ½ cup heavy cream
- 1TAblespoon olive oil
- ½ teaspoon cumin, ground
- 1TEAspoon sweet paprika
- 5garlic cloves, chopped
- 1Cup chicken stock
- A pinch of salt and black pepper

## DIRECTIONS

1.      In a blender, mix the cilantro with the lime juice and the other ingredients except the chicken and the stock and pulse well.

2.      Put the chicken, stock and sauce in the air fryer's pan, toss, introduce the pan in the fryer and cook at 380 degrees F for 25 minutes.

3.      Divide the mix between plates and serve

NUTRITION: Calories 261, Fat 12, Fiber 7, Carbs 15, Protein 25

416. Turkey Chili Preparation time: 10 minutes Cooking time: 25 minutes Servings: 4

## INGREDIENTS

•       1POund turkey breast, skinless, boneless and cubed

•       1Red onion, chopped

•       1Red chili pepper, minced

•       1Cup tomato sauce

•       1TEAspoon chili powder

- Salt and black pepper to the taste
- 1TEAspoon cumin, ground
- 1Cup chicken stock

## DIRECTIONS

1. In a pan that fits your air fryer, mix the turkey with the onion and the other ingredients, stir, introduce in the fryer and cook at 380 degrees F for 25 minutes.

2. Divide into bowls and serve.

NUTRITION: Calories 251, Fat 8, Fiber 8, Carbs 15, Protein 17

417. Chicken and Chickpeas Preparation time: 10 minutes Cooking time: 25 minutes Servings: 4

INGREDIENTS:

- 1POund chicken breast, skinless, boneless and cubed
- 1Cup canned chickpeas, drained
- 1Cup tomato sauce
- Salt and black pepper to the taste

- 2teaspoons olive oil
- ½ teaspoon garlic powder
- ½ teaspoon coriander, ground
- 1TEAspoon basil, dried
- 1TAblespoon parsley, chopped

## DIRECTIONS

1. In the air fryer's pan, mix the chicken with the chickpeas and the other ingredients, toss, introduce the pan in the fryer and cook at 370 degrees F for 25 minutes.

2. Divide the mix into bowls and serve.

NUTRITION: Calories 261, Fat 8, Fiber 6, Carbs 16, Protein 16

minutes Cooking time: 20 minutes Servings: 4

## INGREDIENTS

- 2pounds turkey breast, skinless, boneless and cubed
- 1Cup canned lentils, drained

- ½ cup chicken stock
- ½ teaspoon sweet paprika
- Salt and black pepper to the taste
- 4garlic cloves, minced
- ½ cup cilantro, chopped

DIRECTIONS

1.     In a pan that fits your air fryer, mix the turkey with the lentils and the other ingredients, toss, introduce in the fryer and cook at 380 degrees F for 20 minutes.

2.     Divide everything between plates and serve.

NUTRITION: Calories 261, Fat 7, Fiber 5, Carbs 15, Protein 16

## 419. Meatballs and Sauce Preparation time: 10 minutes Cooking time: 20 minutes

Servings: 4

## INGREDIENTS

* 1POund chicken breast, skinless, boneless and ground
* 2eggs, whisked
* 1Red onion, chopped
* 1TAblespoon cilantro, chopped
* 1TAblespoon chives, chopped
* ½ cup almond flour
* 4garlic cloves, minced
* Salt and black pepper to the taste
* 1Cup tomato sauce
* 1TEAspoon oregano, dried

## DIRECTIONS

1. In a bowl, mix the chicken with the eggs, onion, and the other ingredients except the oregano and tomato sauce, stir and shape medium meatballs out of this mix.

2. In the air fryer's pan, mix the meatballs with the remaining ingredients, and cook at 380 degrees F for 20 minutes.

3. Divide the mix between plates and serve.


NUTRITION: Calories 261, Fat 7, Fiber 6, Carbs 15, Protein 18

420. Ground Turkey Mix Preparation time: 10 minutes Cooking time: 20 minutes Servings: 4
INGREDIENTS

- 2pounds turkey breast, skinless, boneless and ground
- 1Red bell pepper, chopped
- 1Green bell pepper, chopped
- 4spring onions, chopped
- 1Yellow onion, sliced
- 1TEAspoon basil, dried

- 1Cup tomato sauce
- 1TAblespoon soy sauce
- Salt and black pepper to the taste
- 1TAblespoon parsley, chopped

DIRECTIONS

1.    In the air fryer's pan, mix the turkey with the peppers and the other ingredients, introduce the pan in the fryer and cook at 370 degrees F for 20 minutes.

2.    Divide into bowls and serve hot.

NUTRITION: Calories 281, Fat 8, Fiber 5, Carbs 15, Protein 20

421. Chicken and Bacon Mix Preparation time: 10 minutes Cooking time: 25 minutes Servings: 4

INGREDIENTS

A.  2pounds chicken breast, skinless, boneless and cubed

B.  1cup bacon, cooked and chopped

C.  1cup cherry tomatoes, halved

D.  1TAblespoon olive oil

E.  1TAblespoon balsamic vinegar

F.  2scallions, chopped

G.  ½ teaspoon oregano, dried

H.  1TEAspoon sweet paprika

I.  Salt and black pepper to the taste

J.  1TAblespoon cilantro, chopped

## DIRECTIONS

1.      Heat up a pan that fits your air fryer with the oil over medium heat, add the scallions and the meat and brown for 5 minutes.

2.      Add the rest of the ingredients, toss, introduce the pan in the fryer and cook at 380 degrees F for 20 minutes.

3.      Divide everything between plates and serve.

Nutrition: Calories 281, Fat 11, Fiber 5, Carbs 17, Protein 20

422. Turkey and Mango Mix Preparation time: 10 minutes Cooking time: 30 minutes Servings: 4

INGREDIENTS

- 2pounds turkey breast, skinless, boneless and cubed
- 1Cup mango, peeled and cubed
- 2tablespoons butter, melted
- 1TEAspoon chili powder
- 1TEAspoon turmeric powder
- Salt and black pepper to the taste
- 1Yellow onion, chopped
- 1TAblespoon cilantro, chopped

DIRECTIONS

1. In the air fryer's pan, mix the turkey with the mango and the other ingredients, transfer the pan to your air fryer and cook at 380 degrees F for 30 minutes.
2. Divide everything between plates and serve.

NUTRITION: Calories 291, Fat 12, Fiber 7, Carbs 20, Protein 22

423. Herbed Turkey Preparation time: 10 minutes Cooking time: 30 minutes Servings: 6

## INGREDIENTS

- 1POund turkey breast, skinless, boneless and sliced
- 1TAblespoon basil, chopped
- 1TAblespoon coriander, chopped
- 1TAblespoon oregano, chopped
- 1TAblespoon olive oil
- ½ cup chicken stock
- Juice of 1 lime
- Salt and black pepper to the taste

## DIRECTIONS

1. In the air fryer's pan, mix the turkey with the basil and the other ingredients and cook at 370 degrees F for 30 minutes.

2. Divide the mix between plates and serve.

NUTRITION: Calories 281, Fat 7, Fiber 8, Carbs 20, Protein 28

424. Chicken Wings and Sprouts Preparation time: 10 minutes Cooking time: 25 minutes

Servings: 4

INGREDIENTS

- 2pounds chicken wings, halved
- 1cup Brussels sprouts, trimmed and halved
- 1cup tomato sauce
- 1TEAspoon hot sauce
- Salt and black pepper to the taste
- 1TEAspoon coriander, ground
- 1TEAspoon cumin, ground
- 1TAblespoon cilantro, chopped

DIRECTIONS

1. In the air fryer's pan, mix the chicken with the sprouts and the other ingredients, toss, cook at 380 degrees F for 25

minutes, divide between plates and serve.

NUTRITION: Calories 271, Fat 7, Fiber 6, Carbs 14, Protein 20

425. Thyme Turkey Preparation time: 10 minutes Cooking time: 30 minutes Servings: 4

INGREDIENTS

- 2pounds turkey breast, skinless, boneless and cubed
- 2tablespoons thyme, chopped
- Juice of 1 lime
- 1TEAspoon olive oil
- Salt and black pepper to the taste
- 2tablespoons tomato paste
- ½ cup chicken stock
- 1TAblespoon chives, chopped


DIRECTIONS


1. In the air fryer's pan, mix the turkey with the thyme and the other ingredients, introduce the pan in the air fryer and cook at 380 degrees F for 30 minutes.

2. Divide the mix between plates and serve.


NUTRITION: Calories 271, Fat 11, Fiber 7, Carbs

17, Protein 20

# Vegetables Recipes

# 576. Creamy Green Beans and Walnuts

Preparation time: 5 minutes Cooking time: 20 minutes Servings: 4

INGREDIENTS

- 1POund green beans, trimmed and halved
- 1Cup walnuts, chopped
- 2cups cherry tomatoes, halved
- 2tablespoons olive oil
- A pinch of salt and black pepper
- 1TAblespoon chives, chopped

DIRECTIONS

1. In a pan that fits the air fryer, mix the green beans with the walnuts and the other ingredients, toss, put the pan in the air fryer and cook at 380 degrees F for 20 minutes.

2. Divide between plates and serve.

NUTRITION: Calories 141, Fat 3, Fiber 2, Carbs 4, Protein 5

## 577. Garlic Corn Preparation time: 5 minutes Cooking time: 15 minutes Servings: 4

INGREDIENTS

- 2cups corn
- 3garlic cloves, minced
- 1TAblespoon olive oil
- Juice of 1 lime
- 1TEAspoon sweet paprika
- Salt and black pepper to the taste
- 2tablespoons dill, chopped

DIRECTIONS

1. In a pan that fits the air fryer, mix the corn with the garlic and the other ingredients, toss, put the pan in the machine and cook at 390 degrees F for 15 minutes.

2. Divide everything between plates and serve.

NUTRITION: Calories 180, Fat 3, Fiber 2, Carbs 4, Protein 6

578. Green Beans Salad Preparation time: 5 minutes Cooking time: 20 minutes Servings: 4

INGREDIENTS

- 1POund green beans, trimmed and halved
- 1Cup baby spinach
- 1Cup baby kale
- 2tablespoons olive oil
- 1Cup corn
- 1TAblespoon lime juice
- A pinch of salt and black pepper

- 1TEAspoon rosemary, dried
- 1TEAspoon chili powder

DIRECTIONS

1. In the air fryer's pan, combine the green beans with the spinach and the other ingredients, toss and cook at 400 degrees F for 20 minutes.

2. Divide into bowls and serve right away.

NUTRITION: Calories 151, Fat 4, Fiber 2, Carbs 4, Protein 6

## 579. Red Cabbage and Tomatoes

Preparation time: 5 minutes Cooking time: 20 minutes Servings: 4

INGREDIENTS

- 1POund red cabbage, shredded
- ½ pound cherry tomatoes, halved
- 2tablespoons olive oil
- Salt and black pepper to the taste
- ½ cup heavy cream
- 1TAblespoon chives, chopped

DIRECTIONS

1. In a pan that fits the air fryer, combine the cabbage with the tomatoes and other ingredients, put

the pan in the air fryer and cook at 390 degrees F for 20 minutes.

2. Divide between plates and serve.

NUTRITION: Calories 173, Fat 5, Fiber 3, Carbs 5, Protein 8

580. Savoy Cabbage Sauté Preparation time: 5 minutes Cooking time: 20 minutes

Servings: 4

INGREDIENTS

- 1POund Savoy cabbage, shredded
- 2scallions, chopped
- 2tablespoons avocado oil
- Juice of 1 lime
- 2spring onions, chopped
- 2tablespoons tomato sauce
- Salt and black pepper to the taste
- 1TAblespoon chives, chopped

## DIRECTIONS

1.　　In a pan that fits your air fryer, mix the cabbage with the scallions and the other ingredients, toss, put the pan in the fryer and cook at 360 degrees F for 20 minutes.

2.　　Divide between plates and serve.

NUTRITION: Calories 163, Fat 4, Fiber 3, Carbs 6, Protein 7

581. Turmeric Kale Preparation time: 5 minutes Cooking time: 20 minutes Servings: 4

## INGREDIENTS

- 1POund baby kale
- 1TEAspoon turmeric powder
- 1Red bell pepper, cut into strips
- 1Red onion, chopped
- 2tablespoons butter, melted
- 1TAblespoon dill, chopped

## DIRECTIONS

1.    In a pan that fits your air fryer, mix the kale with the turmeric and the other ingredients, put the pan in the fryer and cook at 370 degrees F for 20 minutes.

2.    Divide everything between plates and serve.

NUTRITION: Calories 173, Fat 5, Fiber 3, Carbs 6, Protein 7

582. Lemon Fennel Preparation time: 5 minutes Cooking time: 15 minutes Servings: 4

INGREDIENTS

• 3tablespoons butter, melted

• 2fennel bulbs, sliced

• 1TEAspoon turmeric powder

• 1TEAspoon coriander, ground

• 1TAblespoon lemon zest, grated

• Apinch of salt and black pepper

• 1TAblespoon lemon juice

## DIRECTIONS

1.     In the air fryer's pan, mix the fennel with the melted butter and the other ingredients, toss and cook at 350 degrees F for 15 minutes.

2.     Divide between plates and serve.

NUTRITION: Calories 163, Fat 4, Fiber 3, Carbs 5, Protein 6

583. Balsamic Kale Preparation time: 5 minutes Cooking time: 15 minutes Servings: 4

## INGREDIENTS

- 2cups baby kale
- 2scallions, chopped
- Juice of 1 lime

- 1TAblespoon olive oil
- A pinch of salt and black pepper
- 2tablespoons balsamic vinegar
- 1TAblespoon oregano, chopped

## DIRECTIONS

1. In the air fryer's pan, mix the kale with the scallions and the other ingredients, toss and cook at 350 degrees F for 15 minutes.

2. Divide between plates and serve.

NUTRITION: Calories 143, Fat 4, Fiber 3, Carbs 6, Protein 7

584. Coriander Endives Preparation time: 5 minutes Cooking time: 15 minutes Servings: 4

## INGREDIENTS

- 2endives, trimmed and halved
- 1TAblespoon coriander, chopped
- 1TEAspoon sweet paprika
- 2tablespoons olive oil
- A pinch of salt and black pepper
- 2tablespoons white vinegar
- ½ cup almonds, chopped

## DIRECTIONS

1.     In the air fryer's pan, mix the endives with the coriander and the other ingredients, toss, cook at 350 degrees F for 15 minutes, divide between plates and serve.

NUTRITION: Calories 154, Fat 4, Fiber 3, Carbs 6, Protein 7

585. Cheesy Beets

Preparation time: 5 minutes

Cooking time: 30 minutes Servings: 4

## INGREDIENTS

- 2beets, peeled and roughly cut into wedges
- 1Cup mozzarella, shredded
- 1Red onion, sliced
- A pinch of salt and black pepper
- 1TAblespoon lemon juice

- 2tablespoons chives, chopped
- 2tablespoons olive oil

## DIRECTIONS

2.     In the air fryer's basket, mix the beets with the onion and the other ingredients except the cheese, toss and cook at 380 degrees F for 30 minutes.

3.     Divide the corn between platcs and serve with cheese on top.

NUTRITION: Calories 140, Fat 4, Fiber 3, Carbs 5, Protein 7

586. Frying Potatoes Preparation time: 5 minutes Cooking time: 40 minutes Servings: 4

## INGREDIENTS

- 5to 6 medium potatoes
- Olive oil in a spray bottle if possible
- Mill salt
- Freshly ground pepper

DIRECTION:

1.      Wash the potatoes well and dry them.

2.      Brush with a little oil on both sides if not with the oil

3.      Crush some ground salt and pepper on top.

4.      Place the potatoes in the fryer basket

5.      Set the cooking at 190°C for 40 minutes, in the middle of cooking turn the potatoes for even cooking on both sides.

6.      At the end of cooking, remove the potatoes from the basket, cut them in half and slightly scrape the melting potato inside and add only a little butter, and enjoy!

NUTRITION: Calories 365 Fat 17g Carbohydrates 48g Sugars 0.3g Protein 4g Cholesterol 0mg

minutes Cooking time: 20 minutes Servings: 4

INGREDIENTS

•      1POund Brussels sprouts, trimmed and halved

•      ½ pound baby spinach

•      1TAblespoon olive oil

- Juice of 1 lime
- Salt and black pepper to the taste
- 1TAblespoon parsley, chopped

DIRECTIONS:

1. In the air fryer's pan, mix the sprouts with the spinach and the other ingredients, toss, put the pan in the air fryer and cook at 380 degrees F for 20 minutes.

2. Transfer to bowls and serve.

NUTRITION: Calories 140, Fat 3, Fiber 2, Carbs 5, Protein 6

571. Lemon Tomatoes Preparation time: 5 minutes Cooking time: 20 minutes Servings: 4

INGREDIENTS

- 2pounds cherry tomatoes, halved
- 1TEAspoon sweet paprika
- 1TEAspoon coriander, ground
- 2teaspoons lemon zest, grated

- 2tablespoons olive oil
- 2tablespoons lemon juice
- A handful parsley, chopped

## DIRECTIONS

1. In the air fryer's pan, mix the tomatoes with the paprika and the other ingredients, toss and cook at 370 degrees F for 20 minutes.

2. Divide between plates and serve.

NUTRITION: Calories 151, Fat 2, Fiber 3, Carbs 5, Protein 5

572. Tomato and Green Beans Preparation time: 5 minutes Cooking time: 20 minutes

Servings: 4

## INGREDIENTS

- 1POund cherry tomatoes, halved
- ½ pound green beans, trimmed and halved
- Juice of 1 lime

- 1TEASpoon coriander, ground

- 1TEASpoon sweet paprika

- A pinch of salt and black pepper

- 2tablespoons olive oil

## DIRECTIONS

1.   In a pan that fits your air fryer, mix the tomatoes with the green beans and the other ingredients, toss, put the pan in the machine and cook at 380 degrees F for 20 minutes.

2.   Divide between plates and serve.

NUTRITION: Calories 151, Fat 3, Fiber 2, Carbs 4,

Protein 4

573. Tomato and Onions Mix Preparation time: 5 minutes Cooking time: 20 minutes Servings: 4

## INGREDIENTS

- 1POund cherry tomatoes, halved

- 2red onions, sliced

- 2tablespoons avocado oil

- 1TEAspoon hot paprika
- 1TAblespoon olive oil
- 2teaspoons chili powder
- A pinch of salt and black pepper
- 1TAblespoon chives, chopped

DIRECTIONS

1. In a pan that fits your air fryer, mix the tomatoes with the onions and the other

ingredients, put the pan in the fryer and cook at 390 degrees F for 20 minutes.

2. Divide the mix between plates and serve.

NUTRITION: Calories 173, Fat 4, Fiber 2, Carbs 4, Protein 6

574. Kale Salad Preparation time: 5 minutes Cooking time: 15 minutes Servings: 4

INGREDIENTS

- 1POund kale leaves, torn
- 1Cup kalamata olives, pitted and halved
- 1Cup corn
- Salt and black pepper to the taste
- ¼ cup heavy cream
- 1TAblespoon chives, chopped
- 1Cup cherry tomatoes, halved
- Juice of 1 lime

DIRECTIONS

1. In a pan that fits your air fryer, mix the kale with the olives and the other ingredients, toss, put the pan in the fryer and cook at 390 degrees F for 15 minutes.

2. Divide into bowls and serve right away.

NUTRITION: Calories 161, Fat 2, Fiber 2, Carbs 4,

Protein 6

575. Garlic Carrots Preparation time: 5 minutes Cooking time: 20 minutes Servings: 4

INGREDIENTS

- 1TAblespoon avocado oil

- 1POund baby carrots, peeled
- Juice of 1 lime
- ½ teaspoon sweet paprika
- 6garlic cloves, minced
- 1TAblespoon balsamic vinegar
- Salt and black pepper to the taste

DIRECTIONS

1. In a pan that fits the air fryer, combine the carrots with the oil and the other ingredients, toss gently, put the pan in the air fryer and cook at 380 degrees F for 20 minutes.

2. Divide between plates and serve.

NUTRITION: Calories 121, Fat 3, Fiber 2, Carbs 4,

Protein 6

# Dessert and snacks

795. Sweet Zucchini Chips Preparation time: 15 minutes Cooking time: 4 Hours Servings: 8

INGREDIENTS

- 4cups very thin zucchini slices
- 2Tbsp olive oil
- 2tsp sea salt
- 1TBsp granulated erythritol

DIRECTIONS:

1. Preheat your air fryer to 135 degrees F.

2. Toss the thin zucchini slices with the oil, erythritol and sea salt.

3. Place the zucchini on the air fryer tray or in the air fryer basket.

4. Cook for 4 hours, tossing the zucchini occasionally to allow it to dehydrate evenly.

5. Once crisp, remove the zucchini from the air fryer and enjoy!

NUTRITION: Calories 40, Total Fat 4g, Saturated Fat 0g, Total Carbs 6g, Net Carbs 5g, Protein 1G, Sugar 4g, Fiber 1G, Sodium 570mg, Potassium 0g

796. Cucumber Chips Preparation time: 15 minutes Cooking time: 3 Hours Servings: 4

INGREDIENTS

- 4cups very thin cucumber slices
- 2Tbsp apple cider vinegar
- 2tsp sea salt

DIRECTIONS:

1. Preheat your air fryer to 200 degrees F.

2. Place the cucumber slices on a paper towel and layer another paper towel on top to absorb the moisture in the cucumbers.

3. Place the dried slices in a large bowl and toss with the vinegar and salt.

4. Place the cucumber slices on a tray lined with parchment and then bake in the air fryer for 3 hours. The cucumbers will begin to curl and brown slightly.

5. Turn off the air fryer and let the cucumber slices cool inside the fryer (this will help them dry a little more).

6. Enjoy right away or store in an airtight container.

NUTRITION: Calories 15, Total Fat 0g, Saturated Fat 0g, Total Carbs 4g, Net Carbs 3g, Protein 1G, Sugar 2g, Fiber 1G, Sodium 34mg, Potassium 0g

## 797. Dill and Onion Cucumber Chips

Preparation time: 15 minutes Cooking time: 3 Hours Servings: 4

INGREDIENTS

- 4cups very thin cucumber slices
- 2Tbsp apple cider vinegar
- 2tsp sea salt
- 1TSP dried dill
- 1TSP ground onion powder

DIRECTIONS:

1. Preheat your air fryer to 200 degrees F.
2. Place the cucumber slices on a paper towel and layer another paper towel on

top to absorb the moisture in the cucumbers.

3.    Place the dried slices in a large bowl and toss with the vinegar, dried dill, onion powder and salt.

4.    Place the cucumber slices on a tray lined with parchment and then bake in the air fryer for 3 hours. The cucumbers will begin to curl and brown slightly.

5.    Turn off the air fryer and let the cucumber slices cool inside the fryer (this will help them dry a little more).

6.    Enjoy right away or store in an airtight container.

NUTRITION: Calories 17, Total Fat 0g, Saturated Fat 0g, Total Carbs 4g, Net Carbs 3g, Protein 1G, Sugar 2g, Fiber 1G, Sodium 34mg, Potassium 0g

798.  Smokey Cucumber Chips Preparation time: 15 minutes Cooking time: 3 Hours

Servings: 4

INGREDIENTS

•    4cups very thin cucumber slices

•    2Tbsp apple cider vinegar

•    2tsp smoked sea salt

## DIRECTIONS:

1. Preheat your air fryer to 200 degrees F.

2. Place the cucumber slices on a paper towel and layer another paper towel on top to absorb the moisture in the cucumbers.

3. Place the dried slices in a large bowl and toss with the vinegar and salt.

4. Place the cucumber slices on a tray lined with parchment and then bake in the air fryer for 3 hours. The cucumbers will begin to curl and brown slightly.

5. Turn off the air fryer and let the cucumber slices cool inside the fryer (this will help them dry a little more).

6. Enjoy right away or store in an airtight container.

NUTRITION: Calories 18, Total Fat 0g, Saturated Fat 0g, Total Carbs 4g, Net Carbs 3g, Protein 1G, Sugar 2g, Fiber 1G, Sodium 34mg, Potassium 0g

799. Garlic Parmesan Cucumber Chips

Preparation time: 15 minutes Cooking time: 3 Hours Servings: 4

## INGREDIENTS

- 4cups very thin cucumber slices
- 2Tbsp apple cider vinegar
- 2tsp sea salt
- 1TSP garlic powder
- ¼ cup parmesan cheese

## DIRECTIONS:

1. Preheat your air fryer to 200 degrees F.

2. Place the cucumber slices on a paper towel and layer another paper towel on top to absorb the moisture in the cucumbers.

3. Place the dried slices in a large bowl and toss with the vinegar, garlic powder, parmesan, and salt.

4. Place the cucumber slices on a tray lined with parchment and then bake in the air fryer for 3 hours. The cucumbers will begin to curl and brown slightly.

5. Turn off the air fryer and let the cucumber slices cool inside the fryer (this will help them dry a little more).

6. Enjoy right away or store in an airtight container.

NUTRITION: Calories 34, Total Fat 1G, Saturated Fat 0g, Total Carbs 5g, Net Carbs 4g, Protein 1G, Sugar 3g, Fiber 1G, Sodium 34mg, Potassium 0g


800. Sea Salt and Black Pepper Cucumber Chips


Preparation time: 15 minutes Cooking time: 3 Hours Servings: 4

INGREDIENTS


- 4cups very thin cucumber slices
- 2Tbsp apple cider vinegar
- 2tsp sea salt
- 1TSP ground black pepper


DIRECTIONS:


1.      Preheat your air fryer to 200 degrees F.

2.      Place the cucumber slices on a paper towel and layer another paper towel on top to absorb the moisture in the cucumbers.

3.      Place the dried slices in a large bowl and toss with the vinegar, ground black pepper, and salt.

4.    Place the cucumber slices on a tray lined with parchment and then bake in the air fryer for 3 hours. The cucumbers will begin to curl and brown slightly.

5.    Turn off the air fryer and let the cucumber slices cool inside the fryer (this will help them dry a little more).

6.    Enjoy right away or store in an airtight container.

NUTRITION:Calories 16, Total Fat 0g, Saturated Fat 0g, Total Carbs 4g, Net Carbs 3g, Protein 1G, Sugar 2g, Fiber 1G, Sodium 34mg, Potassium 0g

801.  Taco Cucumber Chips

Preparation time: 15 minutes

Cooking time: 3 Hours Servings: 4 INGREDIENTS
•      4cups very thin cucumber slices
•      2Tbsp apple cider vinegar
•      2tsp sea salt
•      2tsp taco seasoning

DIRECTIONS:

1.      Preheat your air fryer to 200 degrees F.

2.      Place the cucumber slices on a paper towel and layer another paper towel on top to absorb the moisture in the cucumbers.

3.      Place the dried slices in a large bowl and toss with the vinegar, taco seasoning, and salt.

4.      Place the cucumber slices on a tray lined with parchment and then bake in the air fryer for 3 hours. The cucumbers will begin to curl and brown slightly.

5.      Turn off the air fryer and let the cucumber slices cool inside the fryer (this will help them dry a little more).

6.      Enjoy right away or store in an airtight container.

NUTRITION: Calories 23, Total Fat 0g, Saturated Fat 0g, Total Carbs 4g, Net Carbs 3g, Protein 1G,

786. Cayenne Zucchini Chips Preparation time: 15 minutes Cooking time: 4 Hours

Servings: 8

## INGREDIENTS

- 4cups very thin zucchini slices
- 2Tbsp olive oil
- 2tsp sea salt
- 1TSP cayenne pepper

## DIRECTIONS:

1. Preheat your air fryer to 135 degrees F.

2. Toss the thin zucchini slices with the oil, cayenne and sea salt.

3. Place the zucchini on the air fryer tray or in the air fryer basket.

4. Cook for 4 hours, tossing the zucchini occasionally to allow it to dehydrate evenly.

5. Once crisp, remove the zucchini from the air fryer and enjoy!

NUTRITION: Calories 42, Total Fat 4g, Saturated Fat 0g, Total Carbs 3g, Net Carbs 2g, Protein 1G, Sugar 2g, Fiber 1G, Sodium 575mg, Potassium 0g

## 787. Salt and Vinegar Zucchini Chips

Preparation time: 15 minutes Cooking time: 4 Hours Servings: 8

INGREDIENTS

- 4cups very thin zucchini slices
- 2Tbsp olive oil
- 2tsp sea salt
- 1TBsp white balsamic vinegar

DIRECTIONS:

1. Preheat your air fryer to 135 degrees F.

2. Toss the thin zucchini slices with the oil, vinegar and sea salt.

3. Place the zucchini on the air fryer tray or in the air fryer basket.

4. Cook for 4 hours, tossing the zucchini occasionally to allow it to dehydrate evenly.

5. Once crisp, remove the zucchini from the air fryer and enjoy!

NUTRITION: Calories 42, Total Fat 4g, Saturated Fat 0g, Total Carbs 3g, Net Carbs 2g, Protein 1G, Sugar 2g, Fiber 1G, Sodium 570mg, Potassium 0g

788. Smoked Zucchini Chips Preparation time: 15 minutes Cooking time: 4 Hours

Servings: 8

INGREDIENTS

- 4cups very thin zucchini slices
- 2Tbsp olive oil
- 2tsp smoked sea salt

DIRECTIONS:

1.     Preheat your air fryer to 135 degrees F.

2.     Toss the thin zucchini slices with the oil and smoked sea salt.

3.     Place the zucchini on the air fryer tray or in the air fryer basket.

4.     Cook for 4 hours, tossing the zucchini occasionally to allow it to dehydrate evenly.

5.     Once crisp, remove the zucchini from the air fryer and enjoy!

NUTRITION: Calories 40, Total Fat 4g, Saturated Fat 0g, Total Carbs 3g, Net Carbs 2g, Protein 1G, Sugar 2g, Fiber 1G, Sodium 570mg, Potassium 0g

789. Yellow Zucchini Chips Preparation time: 15 minutes Cooking time: 4 Hours

Servings: 8

INGREDIENTS

• 4cups very thin yellow zucchini slices

• 2Tbsp olive oil

• 2tsp sea salt

DIRECTIONS:

1.     Preheat your air fryer to 135 degrees F.

2.     Toss the thin zucchini slices with the oil and sea salt.

3.     Place the zucchini on the air fryer tray or in the air fryer basket.

4.     Cook for 4 hours, tossing the zucchini occasionally to allow it to dehydrate evenly.

5.     Once crisp, remove the zucchini from the air fryer and enjoy!

NUTRITION: Calories 45, Total Fat 4g, Saturated Fat 0g, Total Carbs 3g, Net Carbs 2g, Protein 1G, Sugar 2g, Fiber 1G, Sodium 570mg, Potassium 0g

790. Soft Pretzels Preparation time: 15 minutes Cooking time: 14 minutes Servings: 6

INGREDIENTS

- 2cups almond flour
- 1TBsp baking powder
- 1TSP garlic powder
- 1TSP onion powder
- 3eggs
- 5tbsp softened cream cheese
- 3cups mozzarella cheese, grated
- 1TSP sea salt

DIRECTIONS:

1.	Preheat your air fryer to 400 degrees F and prepare the air fryer tray with parchment paper.


2.	Place the almond flour, onion powder, baking powder and garlic powder in a large bowl and stir well.

3.	Combine the cream cheese and mozzarella in a separate bowl and melt in the microwave, heating slowly and stirring several times to ensure the cheese melts and does not burn.

4.	Add two eggs to the almond flour mix along with the melted cheese. Stir well until a dough forms.

5.	Divide the dough into six equal pieces and roll into your desired pretzel shape.

6.	Place the pretzels on the prepared sheet tray.

7.	Whisk the remaining eggs and brush over the pretzels then sprinkle them all with the sea salt.

8.	Bake in the air fryer for 12 minutes or until the pretzels are golden brown.

9.	Remove from the air fryer and enjoy while warm!


NUTRITION: Calories 449, Total Fat 36g, Saturated Fat 7g, Total Carbs 10g, Net Carbs 6g, Protein 28, Sugar 3g, Fiber 4g, Sodium 234mg, Potassium 48g

## 791. Soft Garlic Parmesan Pretzels

Preparation time: 15 minutes Cooking time: 14 minutes Servings: 6

INGREDIENTS

- 2cups almond flour
- 1Tbsp baking powder
- 1tsp garlic powder
- 1tsp onion powder
- 3eggs
- 5Tbsp softened cream cheese
- 3cups mozzarella cheese, grated
- 1tsp sea salt
- ½ tsp garlic powder

- ¼ cup parmesan cheese

DIRECTIONS:

1.    Preheat your air fryer to 400 degrees F and prepare the air fryer tray with parchment paper.

2.     Place the almond flour, onion powder, baking powder and 1 tsp garlic powder in a large bowl and stir well.

3.     Combine the cream cheese and mozzarella in a separate bowl and melt in the microwave, heating slowly and stirring several times to ensure the cheese melts and does not burn.

4.     Add two eggs to the almond flour mix along with the melted cheese. Stir well until a dough forms.

5.     Divide the dough into six equal pieces and roll into your desired pretzel shape.

6.     Place the pretzels on the prepared sheet tray.

7.     Whisk the remaining eggs and brush over the pretzels then sprinkle them all with the sea salt, parmesan, and ½ tsp garlic powder.

8.     Bake in the air fryer for 12 minutes or until the pretzels are golden brown.

9.     Remove from the air fryer and enjoy while warm!


NUTRITION: Calories 493, Total Fat 39g, Saturated Fat 8g, Total Carbs 10g, Net Carbs 6g, Protein 28, Sugar 3g, Fiber 4g, Sodium 234mg, Potassium 48g


792. Soft Cinnamon Pretzels Preparation time: 15 minutes Cooking time: 14 minutes Servings: 6

INGREDIENTS

- 2cups almond flour
- 1Tbsp baking powder

- 1tsp salt
- 3eggs
- 5Tbsp softened cream cheese
- 3cups mozzarella cheese, grated
- ½ tsp ground cinnamon

## DIRECTIONS:

1.    Preheat your air fryer to 400 degrees F and prepare the air fryer tray with parchment paper.

2.    Place the almond flour, baking powder and salt in a large bowl and stir well.

3.    Combine the cream cheese and mozzarella in a separate bowl and melt in the microwave, heating slowly and stirring several times to ensure the cheese melts and does not burn.

4.    Add two eggs to the almond flour mix along with the melted cheese. Stir well until a dough forms.

5.    Divide the dough into six equal pieces and roll into your desired pretzel shape.

6.    Place the pretzels on the prepared sheet tray.

7.    Whisk the remaining eggs and brush over the pretzels then sprinkle them all with the cinnamon.

8.    Bake in the air fryer for 12 minutes or until the pretzels are golden brown.

9.    Remove from the air fryer and enjoy while warm!


NUTRITION: Calories 432, Total Fat 34g, Saturated Fat 7g, Total Carbs 10g, Net Carbs 6g, Protein 28, Sugar 3g, Fiber 4g, Sodium 212mg, Potassium 48g


793. Soft Pecan Pretzels Preparation time: 15 minutes Cooking time: 14 minutes Servings: 6


## INGREDIENTS

- 2cups almond flour
- 1TBsp baking powder
- 1TSP garlicpowder
- 1TSP onionpowder
- 3eggs
- 5Tbsp softened cream cheese
- 3cups mozzarella cheese, grated

- 1TSP sea salt

- ¼ cup chopped pecans

DIRECTIONS:

1.    Preheat your air fryer to 400 degrees F and prepare the air fryer tray with parchment paper.

2.    Place the almond flour, onion powder, baking powder and garlic powder in a large bowl and stir well.

3.    Combine the cream cheese and mozzarella in a separate bowl and melt in the microwave, heating slowly and stirring several times to ensure the cheese melts and does not burn.

4.    Add two eggs to the almond flour mix along with the melted cheese. Stir well until a dough forms.

5.    Divide the dough into six equal pieces and roll into your desired pretzel shape.

6.    Place the pretzels on the prepared sheet tray.

7.    Whisk the remaining eggs and brush over the pretzels then sprinkle them all with the sea salt and chopped pecans

8.    Bake in the air fryer for 12 minutes or until the pretzels are golden brown.

9.    Remove from the air fryer and enjoy while warm!

NUTRITION: Calories 512, Total Fat 41G, Saturated Fat 10g, Total Carbs 10g, Net Carbs 6g, Protein 31G, Sugar 3g, Fiber 4g, Sodium 234mg, Potassium 48g

## 794. Soft Cheesy Pretzels Preparation time: 15 minutes Cooking time: 14 minutes Servings: 6

INGREDIENTS

- 2cups almond flour
- 1TBsp baking powder
- 1TBsp grated parmesan cheese
- 1TSP garlic powder
- 3eggs
- 5Tbsp softened cream cheese
- 3cups mozzarella cheese, grated
- 1TSP sea salt
- ½ grated cheddar cheese

DIRECTIONS:

1.      Preheat your air fryer to 400 degrees F and prepare the air fryer tray with parchment paper.

2.      Place the almond flour, parmesan, baking powder and garlic powder in a large bowl and stir well.

3.      Combine the cream cheese and mozzarella in a separate bowl and melt in the microwave, heating slowly and stirring several times to ensure the cheese melts and does not burn.

4.      Add two eggs to the almond flour mix along with the melted cheese. Stir well until a dough forms.

5.      Divide the dough into six equal pieces and roll into your desired pretzel shape.

6.      Place the pretzels on the prepared sheet tray.

7.      Whisk the remaining eggs and brush over the pretzels then sprinkle them all with the sea salt and the grated cheddar cheese.

8.      Bake in the air fryer for 12 minutes or until the pretzels are golden brown.

9.      Remove from the air fryer and enjoy while warm!

NUTRITION: Calories 513, Total Fat 40g, Saturated Fat 10g, Total Carbs 10g, Net Carbs 6g, Protein 28, Sugar 3g, Fiber 4g, Sodium 234mg, Potassium 48g

CPSIA information can be obtained
at www.ICGtesting.com
Printed in the USA
LVHW082008240121
677374LV00006B/233

9 781801 592840